Natural
Western Riding

Natural
Western Riding

Don Blazer

Illustrated with Photographs

HOUGHTON MIFFLIN COMPANY BOSTON

For information about permission to reproduce selections from
this book, write to Permissions, Houghton Mifflin Company,
2 Park Street, Boston, Massachusetts 02108.

Library of Congress Cataloging in Publication Data

Blazer, Don, date
Natural western riding.
1. Western riding.   I. Title.
SF309.3.B57   798'.23   79-9204
ISBN 0-395-28476-7

Printed in the United States of America

HAD 15 14 13 12 11 10 9 8 7

TO CATHY

who understands the "how" and "why"
of natural western riding, and thereby
makes its performance an art

Contents

Introduction

TODAY, we are moving away from the art of authentic western riding. I don't know whether it is because we fail to remember its purpose or, as we become more sophisticated, we are embarrassed by its short history.

If our failure is an honest, but mistaken, endeavor to improve our horsemanship, to become more classic in our style, then there is a chance to save western riding. On the other hand, if we continue in our present direction without recognizing the error, future riders will never know and appreciate the way true western riding should be practiced but will accept borrowed, artificial standards.

True western riding was developed by the American cowboy, who lived it until it was almost a faultless art. He was not the originator of the style, but he perfected it.

The American cowboy was a peon, a laborer, a drifter, who lived by his horse and because of his horse. He did not rely on his knowledge of anatomy, equine or otherwise, to control the horse, for he undoubtedly had none. He did not apply the techniques of dressage or any other scientific interpretation of correct aids to instruct his horse, for he was not even aware of their existence. He had neither the desire nor the time to practice horsemanship for its beauty and sophistication or to pursue the pleasure of riding as an art form.

He did not adopt the European horseman's idea of man's superiority and the horse's inferiority.

And because he did not, he unintentionally discovered the secret of his art.

He formed a partnership with his horse. He controlled and directed when he was most capable of making the decisions, but he capitulated to the horse each time the horse was the partner with the greater talent.

Since the cowboy was at work with a partner, he interfered as little as possible with his able companion. The horse was not a servant. Man and horse worked as a team, neither one capable of success or survival without the other.

Fortunately, the art of western riding still exists. It can be seen on occasion at cutting shows, at rodeos, or on ranches where horses work and are worked. And because it is still alive, there is a chance to recapture its original style, the truth, instead of a glamorized image of what never was.

However, the idea of encouraging the partnership between man and horse as the purpose of western riding is fast disappearing. Today, riding experts instruct western riders to use a balanced seat and the upright equitation position and to adopt standards and ideas which are not suited to the intent and purpose of the equipment and animal being used.

The advice they offer does not make better riders. It simply produces western riders who conform to exploited images of what western riding should look like. Certainly the riders don't lack talent. They are merely willing to accept a lower level of perfection in return for a blue ribbon. As an example, modern riders have been taught to adopt a stiff body position in the western saddle. This position restricts the horse's working ability, even though it may give the rider a stock-seat equitation medal.

It is unfortunate that the majority of today's western riders are willing to allow the natural brilliance of the working western horse to be dulled in return for the gloss of saddles gleaming with silver, championship blankets, and a boring, but technically flawless, trip around the show rail.

But the animal's energy is still there under the expensive and heavily merchandised facade, waiting to be used. The horse may have been trained into submissiveness, but his fire can be rekindled.

The horse's intelligence, stamina, quickness, and desire to please can glow again if future riders are willing to strip away meaningless silver and gimmicks, borrowed riding styles, and well-intentioned but misapplied ideals.

This book is for those who wish to reestablish an equal partnership between man and horse, to experience the exhilaration and the joyous harmony of mount and rider which exemplifies western riding as it is meant to be.

Natural
Western Riding

The rider asks the horse for a particular movement, rather than trying to control body position with restrictive force.

1

Taking a Natural Seat

WESTERN riding is not classical dressage, or park seat, or hunt seat. It was never intended to be.

Western riding began as an adaptation to need, just as all riding styles have done. In the case of western riding, it was the need of the working cowboy to use his horse to herd cattle, to move with great flexibility and speed. To do this, the horse needed a certain amount of freedom.

In some respects, this freedom runs counter to the classic style of horsemanship, in which the rider dictates all the horse's movements by giving subtle, controlled cues and receiving subtle, controlled responses, if the horse is well disciplined.

The western rider must likewise ask for a response by giving a subtle cue, but then he must relinquish control, leaving the movement of the horse to the horse, a willing, free spirit.

The results of the two styles are as different as the concepts, and correctly so.

Both styles represent skill and patience and the achievement of the desired response. Neither style is better or worse than the other, and neither is more important or more valuable. If honestly practiced, each style gives its own reward. The styles should not copy one another, but should follow different paths. And so they do.

If the rider is turning to the left, he leads the horse by leaning to the left. The horse follows, moving under rider's weight.

The greatest single difference between the classic style of riding and western riding is that the western rider's goal should not be attempting to remain in the center of his horse. Staying in the center point of a western horse at work is an impossibility. Attempting to do so is an interference. The horse's action is simply too fast.

The rider of a responsive western horse must anticipate and lead the horse with a weight-shift cue. If in turning to the right, the rider leans right, thus leading the horse, the responsive horse will move to the rider's weight, bringing them back into balance.

If the rider asks for a response from the horse, then attempts to remain in the center of the horse, he will undoubtedly find himself behind the horse's movement, interfering with the horse in an attempt to catch up.

The rider cannot catch up with the natural action of the western horse unless he restricts that action, slowing it to a pace at which the rider can function. To do so is a violation of the principle of the partnership.

The western horse which is working correctly can perform better on his own. The astute western rider will let him do so, interfering as little as possible with the horse's natural talent.

The western rider, therefore, takes a natural seat.

The rider's body is erect, yet relaxed, and the rider does not, as so many advocate, attempt to push his shoulders back, hold the chin rigidly up, or keep the back of the heels against an imaginary line running down his arched back.

Each rider, like each horse, is an individual. Taking a natural seat on one horse will not be the same as taking a natural seat on another. What one rider considers a natural seat will not be the same as it is for another.

Riding principles remain constant, but their application should never be forced. Straining to reach an artificial position in the saddle is never required.

By taking a natural seat, the western rider finds he is auto-

4

The natural western rider sits straight down on the horse so the rider's weight is on the front portion of the inner thighs.

matically as close to the horse as is possible when a saddle is used. However, even with the large western saddle, the natural-seat rider will discover he is able to feel the horse's movements easily, and, with practice, can soon anticipate the horse's intended movement.

By sitting naturally on the horse, making no special effort to establish a "correct" position, the rider finds it requires no strain on his part to maintain his own natural body carriage. And as the rider gains confidence, he discovers it is not necessary to grip with the knees to stay with the horse, and that, instead, it is much to his advantage to remain relaxed.

Also, by sitting naturally, the rider sits straight down on the horse. This makes the major contact point the front portion of

In order to maintain close contact with the lower leg, the rider must extend the calf muscles, keeping the heel lower than the toe.

the inner thighs rather than the buttocks. The rider's legs are then positioned slightly forward of the torso.

The rider must now establish the closeness of leg contact which is essential to the subtle control of the horse as well as giving the rider a secure seat. To achieve close contact, the rider must keep his heels lower than his toes. To do this, he must extend the calf muscles of the legs. This is difficult for the beginning rider, for the muscles must be conditioned. With practice, however, it becomes effortless and natural.

Once the rider is seated on the front part of the inner thighs, with his heels lower than his toes, he finds he is "with the horse," sensitive to the horse's movements, in balance, and secure.

The rider must sit deep in the saddle, allowing his body weight to be carried by the saddle seat. When seated in a natural, relaxed position, the rider does not put body weight on the stirrups, for to do so is a cue requesting a particular action from the horse. The stirrups are held in place by pressure which originates from the extension of the calf muscles when the heel is dropped lower than the toe. This pressure has nothing to do with the rider's body weight. The western rider can sample such pressure by sitting in a chair, lifting the feet off the floor, and extending the calf muscles. The pressure created can be felt in the balls of the feet, yet it is obvious there is no body weight on the feet.

The rider must not attempt to grip the horse with his knees, as this requires a tensing of the torso muscles, which immediately reduces the suppleness of the rider's body. Once suppleness of the upper body is lost, there is a corresponding increase in the weight of the upper body, making the rider top-heavy. The top-heavy western rider is almost always behind the movement of his horse, an unforgivable sin.

The rider's elbows should be relaxed. The elbows should be at the rider's sides, but not consciously held close to the body. The good western rider will move his elbows forward and back to change the length of the rein or to lead the horse into movement. Restricting elbow movement is contrary to the free flow of the natural seat and flexibility of the rider's upper body.

The rider should never fear changing the rein in the hand if not doing so restricts or forces a static position of the elbow. If the elbow is held stationary, the result is that the horse eventually hits the bit or is unduly bumped by the bit.

Holding the elbows in a fixed position also causes the rider to tense his back muscles, thereby reducing flexibility and damaging the natural seat.

There are two styles of carriage of the western reins. The Texas style, used in the majority of states, requires the use of split reins. The rider accepts the reins by placing them across

In Texas-style reining, the reins enter the hand above the fingers. Many Texas riders keep the hand below saddle horn level.

the upturned palm of his left hand. The left thumb and index finger then grasp the reins, and the hand is then rolled toward the rider's body, bringing the thumb and index finger to the top. The wrist is held straight. There should be no up, down, forward, or backward slant to the hand.

The hand may be held just in front of and below the saddle horn, or it may be held above the saddle horn. When held in front of the saddle horn, there is a natural twist to the rider's shoulder which results in the left shoulder leading the right somewhat. If the hand is held above the saddle horn, there is almost always an upward tilt to the rider's left forearm.

The right hand does not touch the reins when the Texas style is used, and is held either at the rider's waist or, as I prefer, down at the right thigh.

With the California, or old Spanish, style of reining, the rider accepts the reins by placing the palm of his left hand down upon the reins, then grasping them in the thumb and index finger and rolling the hand away from the body so the thumb and index finger are up.

In California-style reining, the reins enter the hand from below. The difference is small, but lowers the reins, thereby lowering the horse's head.

For California reining, the reins are closed and a romal is attached. The romal is held in the right hand, which is carried on the right thigh. Just how far down the romal the rider wants to put his right hand depends on what is most comfortable under the circumstances. Some show association rules prescribe that there will be a minimum distance of 16 inches between the hand holding the reins and the hand on the thigh. This ruling is one of the impractical and artificial standards that have no place in good riding.

In California-style reining, the reining hand is also held in front of, or just above, the saddle horn. The decision is with the rider. However, it is my opinion that it is easier for the horse to maintain a somewhat lower head position if the rein is kept as low as possible. If the rider lets the horse carry his head low, the horse will usually show a little more quickness in turns.

The rider must use his fingers, not his entire hand, when moving the reins to cue or control the horse. Since the rider has grasped the reins between the thumb and index finger, his remaining three fingers are free to play upon the reins. The rider should spread these fingers to a degree, thereby allowing himself the opportunity to shorten, lengthen, or bump the reins with the fingers without the necessity of moving the whole hand or arm.

A rolling action of the wrist is all that should be required to neck-rein the highly polished western horse. Movement of the entire arm may be necessary with the green or even the intermediate horse in order to evoke the correct response. Even under these circumstances, the rider will find the free movement of the fingers is an added advantage.

If it is necessary to shorten or lengthen the reins to a greater degree than can be accomplished through the contraction and relaxation of the fingers, then the rider has the option of twisting the wrist away, or toward, his body or moving his elbow.

Gripping the reins with only the thumb and index finger helps the rider keep his hands light. And as I will repeat again and again, light (good) hands are possessed only by the rider who makes full use of good leg cues.

The rider should not look down unnecessarily, but should always try to be looking in the direction or intended direction of travel. Looking down brings the upper body forward, and while it might make only the slightest degree of change, the sensitive horse will respond, generally by an increase in his speed.

Most often, the rider is tempted to look down for one of two reasons. First, the rider is trying to determine on which lead the horse is working. Second, the rider is trying to locate a stirrup. There is no good excuse for either. The good western rider determines the horse's lead by feel, as I will explain later. The good western rider also knows, through practice and feel, the location of a properly placed stirrup.

The best stirrup length for the natural-seat rider is determined by having the rider sit on the horse with his legs relaxed and hanging at full length. The bottom of the stirrups should be opposite the rider's ankles. In this position, the rider need only lift his toes in order to put his feet in the stirrups.

The bottom of the stirrup should be opposite the rider's ankle. Many western riders use a long stirrup in an attempt to straighten the leg.

As the feet are inserted in the stirrups, the rider should rest them against the inside edge of the stirrups. The pressure against the stirrups should be applied by the balls of the feet. If the rider has lifted his toes in order to place his feet in the stirrups, he will find the toes are somewhat higher than the heels and the calf muscles of the legs are stretched properly. This is the correct position.

If necessary, the rider must punch new holes in the stirrup leathers to obtain the proper length. As ridiculous as it may seem to the serious student, too many riders simply adjust the stirrups to the saddlemaker's predetermined lengths, whether they are correct or not. A good rider will always make the necessary adjustments to keep the stirrup leathers even. Over a

The foot is properly positioned against inside edge of stirrup, heel lower than toe, and contact is with the ball of the foot.

period of time, the left stirrup lengthens from the extra strain encountered in mounting and dismounting.

Having the stirrups at the correct length helps achieve the natural closeness of the rider's body to the horse which is so necessary. It helps the rider sit down on the horse and helps keep the rider in the center of the horse when that position is desired.

When the rider sits in the center of the horse, the rider's spine and the horse's spine are aligned. This is correct when the western horse is at rest or is moving straight forward or straight back. However, the western rider will lean into the direction of travel when turning, and his spine will then be inclined toward the direction of travel. When responding correctly, the western horse will move under, or to, the rider, returning the partnership to balance.

If he is sitting properly on the inside front portion of the thighs, the rider's tailbone will not come against the cantle of the saddle, not even when he leans a little backward and to the inside of a turn, a weight-shift position occasionally used in training the intermediate horse.

By remaining seated in the natural position, the rider finds that when the upper body is inclined in the direction of travel, his legs automatically and naturally move into the proper leg aid positions for the turns.

The natural seat is a relaxed seat. By sitting the natural seat, the western rider can function in harmony with the horse. Force, restrictive stiffness, and artificial standards can be forgotten forever.

2

Tack — Its Choice and Use

THE CHOICE of saddle is important in riding by the natural-western-seat method. An equitation saddle will not do, nor will a cutting saddle or a game saddle. Because form follows function in the design of all equipment, including the western saddle, it is obvious that before selecting a saddle, the rider must decide how the saddle is to be used.

For the western rider who wants to establish a partnership with his horse in performing fast exercises, the ranch saddle and the roper saddle are most acceptable. All other designs are too specialized and inhibit, rather than enhance, the natural western seat.

The equitation saddle is heavily padded in the seat between the swell and the cantle. This padding locks the rider down in the seat, giving him the feeling of being securely set in the proper position. However, when it comes time to work the horse or to free the horse to show his own brilliance, the rider discovers he is still locked into position, decidedly not able to lead, and hardly able to follow, the movements of the horse.

Today's cutting saddle and game saddle are designed exclusively for specific activities. Years ago, cutting was practiced by the cowboys who used an all-purpose ranch saddle, but now the art of cutting is generally reserved for the professional trainer or the dedicated amateur, who demand special assistance from their saddles.

Game saddles are for barrel racers and pole benders. They are cut small and are light, but they lack comfort and sufficient seat size for the working rider.

The roper saddle is functional enough for the natural-seat rider, but its design does create some limitations. A good roper must stand in the stirrups to be in the proper position to catch a steer or calf. Therefore, there is little forward swing to the fenders, which are rather stiff. This rigidity keeps the roper from flopping back to the cantle when shifting to a standing position. So although there is some restriction to leg movement with the roper saddle, there is still sufficient freedom for the natural-seat rider to lead the horse.

The ranch saddle, therefore, remains the best saddle for the rider who wants to flow with the movement of the horse. It has a more flexible fender, allowing greater freedom of leg movement. The seat is more or less in the center of the saddle, with virtually the same slope from the swell as from the cantle, so the rider is pushed neither forward nor back.

Unfortunately, by its style and design, the western saddle does keep the rider a fair distance from the horse, but this disadvantage can be minimized if the saddle fits the horse properly. The best saddle in either the roper or ranch type is one in which the seat is narrow so the rider can easily keep his legs against the horse's sides.

A well-fitting saddle will have sufficient width at the gullet to fit over the horse's withers without applying painful pressure.

The twist of the saddletree determines how the saddle fits the horse's back. If the bars of the saddle are the same in the back as at the gullet, the saddle may fit the withers, but it will be resting on top of the horse's back at the rear. A properly twisted tree will leave the bars narrow at the withers but flat and wide at the rear of the saddle.

A relatively easy and safe test of saddle fit can be made by saddling the horse with a single saddle pad, saddle blanket, and saddle. The horse should be worked until he is warm enough to produce some sweat under the saddle. If the saddle fits properly, when it is removed the sweat on the horse's back will be evenly distributed. If there are dry spots or spots which are excessively wet, then the saddle does not fit well.

In most cases, an ill-fitting saddle can be helped with extra padding. This solution will protect the horse until a properly fitting saddle can be obtained, but it does present the rider with another disadvantage. The heavy padding lifts the saddle and rider away from the horse, putting the rider out of balance.

The overall length of the saddle must also be proper for the length of the horse's back. The rear edge of the saddle jockey must never go far enough back to reach the point of the horse's hip. Short-backed horses should only wear saddles which have had the jockey cut down.

The average rider will normally find a 15-inch saddle seat most desirable. I prefer a little more room, however, and ride a 16-inch saddle. When the action speeds up, the rider needs freedom of movement to lead the horse into the next exercise. Also, it is easier for the rider to make the necessary weight-shift cues and for the horse to recognize such cues. Any restriction in the saddle seat forces the rider into a more rigid, upright position, a position which is ultimately detrimental to both horse and rider.

A smooth swell on the saddle, 12 to 13 inches in width, is most desirable for the western rider who wants to perform a variety of exercises.

All other factors being equal, a lighter saddle of from 30 to 35 pounds makes a better working saddle than one which weighs 40 to 50 pounds. Today's show saddles tend to be bulky and heavy, laden with silver. While I'm not opposed to show-ring glitter, and I certainly understand how eye-catching such silver-appointed saddles can be, I think a clever horseman can

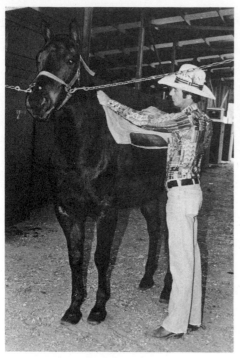

Above, left: Place the saddle blanket or pad well forward. Once the saddle is placed, slide pad and saddle backward, smoothing horse's coat. *Above, right:* Once saddle and pad are in place, be sure to lift pad up into saddle gullet, relieving pressure on the horse's withers. *Bottom:* When cinching, don't try to make it tight with first effort. Allow the horse to relax, then tighten again. Smooth skin under cinch.

have such a saddle designed so it will not be so heavy that it impairs the horse's working ability. A good saddlemaker can produce an excellent saddle without using thick, inflexible leather.

A second cinch on the saddle, originally designed to keep the rear of the saddle from coming up when a roper dallies, is seldom seen in the show ring today, and serves no purpose for the natural-seat rider.

Breast collars are becoming very popular with show-ring riders as another place to put more silver. However, if the saddle fits properly, and if the horse has good conformation and is not overweight, it is not advisable to put a breast collar on a good working horse. There is no way additional straps and weight can be added to the equipment the horse must carry without impairing his natural movement and/or his breathing to some degree. Use a breast collar only if it is necessary to keep the saddle in place on a mutton-withered or low-backed horse.

After taking the horse to the hitching rail or crossties to be saddled, the rider should first clean the horse's feet, then brush the horse down, making sure the hair lies flat and there is no dirt present which might rub against any equipment and cause sores. Then the horse should be saddled before the bridle is put in place.

Place the saddle pad well up over the withers. Then, holding the saddle by the horn and cantle, and facing the rear of the horse, swing the saddle up over the horse's back and gently lower it into place. The saddle should be a little forward of its best position. By moving both the saddle and the saddle pad back into the proper position, you will also be smoothing the hair under the pad.

With the saddle in place, lift the saddle pad up off the withers by pushing it gently into the saddle gullet.

Moving to the horse's right side, release the girth and let it drop down. Return to the horse's left side, reach under and bring the girth up into place so that it can be cinched with the latigo. The girth should be centered under the horse's body, and it should be far enough back so that it does not interfere with the movement of the horse's elbow. Each of the horse's front legs should be pulled forward to smooth the skin under the girth.

Do not try to tighten the girth completely at first. Cinch the horse snugly, then walk him in a small circle several times. Adjust the girth again. I like the girth to be snug, but not tight. You should be able to insert your fingers easily between the girth and the horse.

When bridling the horse, regardless of style of headstall, the rider should insert the bit gently. The bit should first be warmed or cooled to body temperature and, needless to say, should always be clean. Take great care not to strike the horse's teeth.

To insert the bit in the horse's mouth, the rider should grasp the crownpiece of the headstall in the right hand. The left hand is placed under the bit. Standing on the left side of the horse, and facing in the same direction as the horse, the rider uses the thumb of his left hand to open the horse's mouth, while the fingers of the left hand lift and guide the bit into the mouth. The left thumb can be inserted in the corner of the horse's mouth. When the thumb is pressed down on the horse's tongue, the horse will open his mouth to accept the bit.

To steady the horse's head in position for bridling, the rider puts his right hand and arm over the horse's neck and poll. In this position, the rider's arm and hand help keep the horse's head down, making it easier to insert the bit.

With the crownpiece of the headstall near its final position, the bit will hang close to the horse's mouth. Once the bit has been accepted by the horse, the crownpiece can then be slipped over the horse's ears and into place. A one-eared western headstall fits over the horse's right ear. The bit should be positioned in the mouth so that it fits snugly in the corners.

Use extreme caution in bridling the western horse. The western curb bit is big and can easily bump teeth, causing discomfort.

I don't like to see wrinkles at the corners of the horse's mouth.

The physical construction of the mouth and position of the horse's teeth may require the placement of the bit to be adjusted. I like to use the entire length of the bars of the mouth and therefore will regularly adjust the bit placement so the lower, middle, and upper portions of the bars are used. To do so sensitizes the entire length of the bar, and prevents a hardening of the bar in a particular spot. The upper portion of the bar is used if the bit fits snugly into the corners of the mouth. If the corners of the mouth are wrinkled, then the bit is generally too high, frequently even lying against the first molars.

The rider should then smooth the headstall, making sure

The western rider strives for "light" mouth contact, to give the horse confidence, rather than restricting his movement.

there are no twists in the leather and that it fits properly. Once the headstall is in place, the throatlatch, if there is one, should be fastened. The throatlatch should be loose enough to permit flexion without restriction.

The choice of reining styles is up to the rider. He can choose the Texas style of reining or the California style, but neither makes the horse work better or worse. The working ability of the horse is a matter of natural talent and training and is not dependent on the style of reining used by the rider.

Regardless of the reining style, the rider should always have light mouth contact with the well-trained, responsive western horse. This contact reassures the horse and gives him confidence. If the rider releases the reins, removing contact and breaking the lines of communication, the horse either will lose confidence and wander or will assume the decision-making process. Assumption of leadership by the horse is desirable only when both the horse and rider know that the action contemplated requires the horse's superior talent. This occurs when horse and man are working or cutting cattle and occasionally when performing in a reining contest.

The rider who tries to maintain mouth contact and also direct the action when working or cutting cattle is penalized in two ways. First, he will be penalized by the judge, but, more unfortunately, he will penalize himself because his reactions will never be as quick or as instinctive as the horse's.

While light mouth communication must always be maintained, some heavy-handed western riders mistakenly rely on the reins for more than a signal for performance. The reins become a kind of security blanket for balance. As the rider becomes heavier and heavier on the bit, the horse becomes less and less sensitive to the message. The horse cannot concentrate on giving any kind of a performance because he is doing everything he can to escape the pain of the bit that is being banged and bumped in the most tender part of his mouth.

The bit should hang naturally in the horse's mouth. The design and weight of the bit help position the western horse's head. The weight of the western bit helps keep the horse's head low while acting as a direct, responsive line of communication between the animal's mouth and the rider's relaxed, gentle fingers.

When the rider shortens the reins, the bit should move. A quick response by the horse to minimal bit movement indicates that the horse has a sensitive, "made" mouth. Communication has been established and the horse is reacting to the request. The more subtle the request from the rider, the better.

Well-tacked horse

The western horse should always be seeking the center of the reins. A slight increase of pressure on the side of the horse's neck from one rein or the other should generate an immediate response. The horse should attempt to find the center point, an equalization of rein pressure on each side of the neck. When the horse finds this point, the reins will simply be resting alongside the horse's neck.

When asking the horse to turn in a particular direction by neck-reining, there is no backward pull on the reins, therefore no pressure in the horse's mouth caused by a change in the bit position. Almost everyone has seen improper neck-reining in which the horse is asked, for example, to move to the left and, in responding, the horse's head becomes elevated and tilts out to the right. This is caused by the rider's incorrectly pulling back on the reins and failing to use leg and weight-shift aids.

Generally, the well-schooled western horse will work satisfactorily on a low port curb with medium-length shank (5 to 5½ inches). Some western horses will carry their head in a better position with the aid of the heavier half-breed bit. The half-breed has a straight bar rather than a port mouthpiece. A cricket with a roller is mounted on top of the bar mouthpiece of the half-breed bit.

In natural western riding, where leg, weight-shift, and rein aids are correctly employed, a severe bit is never needed. More often than not, the horse will be totally responsive on a gentle, low port curb.

Today's generally accepted artificial standard of stiff, restrictive, unyielding equitation has brought about the use of bits of punishment as a last resort means of forcing the horse to comply. To use a heavier or more severe bit to force a horse into position is a deterioration of horsemanship and is directly opposite to the principles of natural western riding.

Today, there are often classes for the western horse which is ridden on the hackamore (bosal, never a mechanical hackamore). Such classes are normally for junior horses (four years of age or under) which are considered "still in training." There are hackamore pleasure and hackamore reining classes at some shows. Such classes evidence the renewed popularity of leaving horses in a "training device" for a longer period of time rather than rushing them into a bit before they are ready. This interest in the hackamore, I believe, is a positive indication the art of natural western riding is still very important to the serious student.

3

Mounting and Dismounting

THERE are two safe ways to mount and dismount from the western-trained horse. One is a natural-seat method; the other, the equitation-seat procedure.

If you ever intend to show horses and to enter an equitation or horsemanship class, you will be required to use the equitation-seat procedure, so you should know the proper sequence of movement. For all other circumstances, using the equitation mount and dismount is unnecessary and impractical. The movement is stiff and artificial, even though it is safe.

The formal procedure, when used in the show ring, begins with the rider standing quietly at the horse's head, facing in the same direction as the horse. The rider holds the left rein in the right hand. When told to mount, the rider turns toward the horse's head, checks the bit position, the chin strap, and the throatlatch and headstall buckles. The rider then turns and moves toward the horse's hindquarters, releasing the rein from the right hand and grasping it immediately with the left hand. By allowing the rein to slip through the left hand, the rider can move to the center of the horse. The rider must never release the rein, which would mean losing control of the horse.

When the rider reaches the mounting position, the cinch latigo should be checked to make sure the saddle is still snug. The rider will then face the horse's shoulder, shortening the

In "equitation" mounting, the rider faces the horse's hindquarters, turns the stirrup, and uses the right hand on the saddle horn.

Opposite: The rider should keep the right leg as straight as possible when swinging into saddle. The rider's foot should not touch horse.

reins and collecting the romal in the left hand. With the right hand, the rider rotates the stirrup so the left foot can be placed in it while the rider is facing the rear of the horse. The rider then turns toward the horse's hindquarters and places his left foot in the stirrup.

With the right hand, the rider grasps the saddle horn, placing the left hand on the horse's neck just in front of the saddle. The rider takes two little hops on the right foot and lifts himself into standing position in the stirrup, the right foot now being next to the left. The rider should not bend at the waist, which would make him lean over the saddle. The body should be held straight, and all movements, to this point, should be as graceful as possible.

The right leg is now swung over the horse's rump, and every attempt should be made to keep the leg as straight as possible so the horse is not bumped. When the rider is seated, the right foot is slipped into the stirrup. It should not be necessary for the rider to look down to find the stirrup.

Once the rider is seated properly, the romal is moved to the right side by lifting the left hand and reaching under with the right hand to grasp the romal. The romal is brought into position on the right thigh slowly and carefully.

If the rider is using the Texas style of reining, the rider may release the loose ends of the split reins, allowing them to fall on the side of the horse's neck corresponding to the rider's hand which will hold the reins during the performance exercises.

The reins are then adjusted to the proper position for the next requested exercise.

The equitation dismount normally comes at the end of the class when all contestants are in the lineup in the center of the arena.

The first step of the dismount, if the rider is using California-style reins, is to change the position of the romal. The rider raises the left hand and passes the romal under his left hand with the right hand. Then both the reins and the romal are held with the left hand to keep the romal from dropping.

The rider places the right hand on the saddle horn and the left hand on the horse's neck just in front of the saddle, takes the right foot from the stirrup, and swings the right leg over the horse's rump, bringing the right foot down slowly into position next to the left foot.

The rider should hesitate for just a moment at this point, then gracefully lower the right foot to the ground. The left foot is then removed from the stirrup and placed on the ground next to the right foot. The rider should then be standing squarely on both feet, facing the horse's left side.

The closed reins are then released from the grasp of the left hand and allowed to rest on the hore's neck just in front of the saddle. The romal is draped around the saddle horn and across the pommel from the right side to the left so that it lies on the horse's left side, not touching the ground.

If split reins are being used, the rider has the option of leaving the right rein draped across the horse's neck in front of the saddle, or of slipping it under the horse's neck and holding it, and the left rein in the right hand. The rider then moves forward to stand by the horse's head. Once at the horse's head, the rider should stand squarely and quietly, awaiting the judge's instructions.

If closed reins are being used, the rider takes the left rein in the right hand and moves to the horse's head, allowing the rein to slip through the fingers. The rider never lets go of the reins.

Natural-seat mounts and dismounts are not so formal. They are done in a more relaxed manner and are more practical and quite possibly even a little safer.

When mounting, the rider takes the reins in the left hand, shortening them to the point of light mouth contact with the horse.

Two options are open to the rider. The reins can be left an equal length, positioning the horse's head straight forward, or the rider may shorten the left or right rein.

If the left rein is shortened, the horse's head is pulled to the left, and the horse will have a tendency to move his hindquarters away from the rider trying to mount. If the horse should become nervous or shy during mounting, the rider will find the horse moving away and at the same time circling the rider. The danger here may be that a rider could have his left foot caught in the stirrup if the stirrup is too narrow.

If the right rein is shortened, the horse's head is pulled to the right, forcing the horse to move in to the rider. If the horse should spook or shy during mounting, there is the possibility the horse could then knock the rider off balance. However, with the head positioned to the right, the horse will not be able to move away from the rider, making it easier for the rider to mount.

The well-trained western horse should not have to have his head turned in either direction. With a green or nervous horse, however, I personally prefer shortening the left rein, always bringing the horse's forehand to me. I much prefer moving to the horse, rather than having the horse move in to me.

Once the reins are positioned to the satisfaction of the rider for the particular horse being ridden, the rider turns his body so that he is facing in the same direction as the horse. The left foot is then positioned in the stirrup, and with the left hand on the horse's neck and the right hand on the saddle horn, the rider lifts his body by straightening the left leg. The rider should never attempt to pull himself up with his arms.

In "natural" mounting, the rider faces in the same direction as the horse, then lifts the body with the muscles of the left leg.

The rider's right leg is allowed to move slightly back toward the horse's hindquarters and is then swung over the horse's rump and to the horse's right side. The rider sits gently in the saddle, and the right foot is placed in the right stirrup. The rider then positions the reins for the horse's comfort and control.

The dismount is the same procedure in reverse.

The rider must remember not to assume a stiff, upright position but to be as relaxed and supple as possible.

If the rider mounts and dismounts facing in the same direction as the horse, the danger of catching a foot in the stirrup, should the horse move, is eliminated. If the horse should bolt forward, the rider's foot comes out of the stirrup easily since the stirrup is not twisted.

Once he is seated naturally in the saddle, the rider should be able to keep the heels lower than the toes easily by simply extending the calf muscles of the legs. The rider's legs should be directly under his body, or just a bit forward, whichever is most comfortable for the individual rider on that particular horse.

The differences in size, weight, and conformation of horses will make taking the natural seat somewhat different for each rider, for each individual also has special advantages and disadvantages because of size, weight, and length of legs and arms. But when seated naturally, any rider should be able to look down and see the tips of his boots without leaning forward.

The stirrup length should never be so long that the rider is reaching with the legs in order to keep the foot in the stirrup. The stirrups should never be so short that the rider's knee is flexed to the point of blocking a view of the rider's toe.

Generally, the stirrup will be about right when the bottom of the stirrup is even with the inside of the rider's ankle. However, the rider should not be afraid to adjust the stirrups to a length which provides the most freedom and comfort.

The rider should be sitting on the front, inside portion of the thighs. The back should be straight, never arched, and the shoulders squared naturally. When the horse is standing quietly, the rider's upper body is held upright but not inflexible. And with the horse motionless, the reins should be loose, the cue to the horse that no movement is desired.

When he is seated naturally, with arms, hands, legs, and body in the most comfortable arrangement, the rider is in a position to request movement from the horse. But before requesting movement, the rider must inform the horse that a request for action will be forthcoming. He does this by simply lifting the reins and starting to shorten them.

But before continuing with instructions on cues to move the

The natural western rider should not be afraid to adjust stirrups or body position until she is erect, yet completely relaxed.

horse, let's discuss the position of the bit in the horse's mouth. This is most important.

With the western horse, the bit should rest in its natural balance position while the horse is working. (The bit is in its natural position as it hangs from the headstall.) In all other styles of riding, there is direct contact with the horse's mouth from the rider's hands through the reins and bit. But this is not so when the advanced western horse is working. With the advanced western horse, the bit simply rests in the horse's mouth, the reins reasonably loose, and not tipping the natural hang of the bit. There is no mouth contact through the reins until the rider wishes to communicate a new request which requires a new bit position.

In a change of direction without a change of gait, no new position is required, so the rider does not move the bit but simply changes direction with the use of leg, weight, and rein-pressure cues.

If the rider wishes a new gait, a stop, a spin, or any other exercise which requires a new head position by the horse, then — and only then — does the rider communicate through bit pressure.

Once the bit-pressure cue has been acknowledged by the horse, the rider releases the bit pressure immediately and allows the horse to work on his own.

All bit-pressure cues must be subtle. A gentle cue will always suffice. It is not necessary to jerk or bang the bit around in the mouth of a well-schooled western horse.

If the horse, for any reason, should become balky or cranky, the natural western rider never attempts to correct the horse through punishing bit pressure. The rider may shorten the reins, collecting the horse and holding a fixed hand to establish the bit as a restricting force. The rider will then correct the horse through aggressive leg actions.

The length of the reins is an individual matter, determined by the length of the head and neck of the horse, the amount of direct spinal flexion required for the particular exercise to be executed, and the length of the rider's arms and the position of the rider's body. The correct length of the reins will therefore always be slightly different for each horse and each rider. The correct length will be recognized by horse and rider only when they are communicating well and working in harmony. Recognition of correct rein length comes through "feel" and is achieved only after considerable practice.

So, as the rider now lifts the reins and begins to shorten them, the horse will recognize that a request for action is about

The California-style western rider shortens the reins by pulling them through the left hand. The left remains still; right hand works.

to be made. He will become alert and ready his body for the requested activity.

If the rider intends to ask for a walk, he will shorten the reins gently until he feels the first sensation of the weight of the bit. At that point, the rider must stop shortening the reins and lengthen them by one-quarter to one-half inch.

The western horse's body will be at its greatest length when walking, so the rider must not hold a short rein, which is a request for the horse to shorten its body.

With the reins in the correct position, the rider gives the verbal command to walk, then squeezes gently with both legs. The rider should use only his lower legs. With the responsive, advanced horse, it is not necessary, or desirable, to use the heels.

All movement by the horse is initiated with the hindquarters. The leg pressure applied by the rider tells the horse to move the hindquarters forward, to begin driving. The extended rein and lack of bit pressure tell the horse not to collect its body, but to move off at the walk.

The walk is a four-beat gait and the horse moves with its head down, neck extended. Action can start with the left or right hind leg. If the right hind leg moves first, then the right foreleg must move second in order to get out of the way of the right hind, which will overstep the previous contact point of the right foreleg, if the horse is driving well. The left hind leg then moves, followed by the left fore. The right hind immediately begins a new sequence, and the horse is walking.

The jog is a learned gait, rather than a natural one. To move at the jog, the rider gives the voice command "Jog," then shortens the reins until the horse flexes at the poll by shortening his

The walk is a four-beat gait. The good western horse walks out freely, and the good western rider keeps the horse covering ground.

The jog is a two-beat diagonal gait. The horse does not move faster than at a walk, but instead, shortens his stride by lifting his feet.

neck and chest muscles and also flexes his spine by bringing the hindquarters farther under his body. The head is carried in the vertical position.

The rider helps the horse flex at the poll and bend his spine by holding a fixed bit position and squeezing with both legs to drive the horse's hindquarters under the body.

The rider does not pull back on the reins, which would exert much too strong a pressure on the horse's mouth. Instead, the rider shortens the reins gently, holds a fixed bit position, and then pushes the horse to the bit by use of strong leg pressure. When the horse reaches the correct position and relaxes, the bit pressure will have been removed because the horse has shortened his body.

The jog is a diagonal two-beat gait in which one hind leg and the opposite foreleg move together. As they are grounded, the other diagonal legs move together, completing the sequence. The flight of the horse's foot at the jog is higher and more rounded than when the horse is walking.

If the horse jogs slowly, the crisscross movement of the horse's body is relatively easy for the rider to sit. But if the horse moves quickly, the rider will find it most difficult to keep from bouncing without moving his entire body forward or getting behind the horse's center of gravity.

The jog may seem the most difficult gait to sit. But the natural western rider will sit it as he does all gaits, by relaxing the body and taking a deep seat. The heels are lower than the toes because the calf muscles are extended, but the leg is not rigid and the knee is not locked. The rider's back must remain supple and flexible and the shoulders are held square, but not stiff. The chin is up so the rider can look forward, but the neck is not rigid. The side-to-side motion of the jogging horse is absorbed by the rider's pelvic area, which moves with the movement of the horse, thus keeping the upper body from swaying. Problems develop any time the rider stiffens his body.

In western riding, the rider should not move either ahead of or behind the center point of the horse. Instead, he should slow the gait until it is comfortable. The gait can be slowed by gently "bumping" the horse by shortening the reins to apply light bit pressure, then immediately lengthening the reins again. This bumping is sometimes required every two or three strides until the horse learns to adjust his speed and concentrate on the exercise.

The western lope is a three-beat gait in which the action is

The lope is a three-beat gait. The horse must shorten his body and round his stride. The lope is a relaxed, slow-moving gait.

initiated by the opposite hind leg of the lead desired. For example, if the rider wants a right lead, the first movement of the gait will be a short stride by the horse's left hind foot. The second beat is the right hind foot and the left forefoot moving together. The final beat is the right forefoot in an extended stride.

To request the lope, the rider must shorten the reins as a means of telling the horse a new gait, more elevated than the jog, is required. The rider then shifts his weight toward the horse's hindquarters on the left side by simply moving his left hip back, and at the same time applies left leg pressure. This informs the horse that movement by the left hind foot is desired. The rider's weight over the left hind foot causes the horse to take a shortened stride, thus insuring a right lead.

With the less advanced western horse, the rider may also rein the horse just a little to the left, thus exposing the horse's right shoulder.

As the horse lopes along, the rider must maintain his natural, relaxed body position and the slight lower left leg pressure (informing the horse he is to continue on the right lead). After the horse starts to lope, the rider may discontinue any mouth contact by releasing the reins, either by allowing them to slip through his hand or by extending his arm. However, at this gait, the horse may have a tendency to change his head position and the rider must be prepared to correct his partner by bumping with the bit.

To stop the horse from any gait, the rider will give the verbal command "Ho" and will then squeeze with both legs, driving the horse's hindquarters well under the body and pushing the horse to the bit, which will be held in a fixed, unyielding position. At the same time that he is applying firm leg pressure, the rider must tighten his stomach muscles, forcing the pelvis slightly forward. Tightening the stomach muscles keeps the rider's buttocks in the seat of the saddle and keeps him from leaning back.

The rider must never, never jerk back on the reins in an attempt to stop the horse. The horse must be pushed to the fixed bit and must find immediate relief as the stop is completed.

The western horse normally will not stop from a walk or jog with the hind feet squared. To square the hind feet, the rider should shorten the reins until there is mouth contact, then hold a fixed hand so the bit acts as a barrier to forward movement.

If the horse's left hind foot is back, it can be moved forward by applying light pressure with the lower left leg, thus initiating hind foot action. The leg pressure is removed instantly when the horse moves the left hind foot forward.

The rider should be able to determine which foot is extended, or which hind foot is grounded during movement, by the feel of the horse. When the horse is walking, the horse's hip corresponding to the foot which is grounded will be high. Conversely, the hip on the opposite side will be low and that foot will be off the ground.

All the cues for the basic walk, jog, lope, and stop are reinforced by a verbal command. My instructions are actually verbs — "Walk," "Jog," "Lope," and "Ho" for stop. The commands are easily understood by the horse and give the horse the opportunity to perform as requested without the danger of unintentional, premature punishment by the rider.

I use voice commands even in the show ring. Of course, the verbal command is given in a very low, soft tone, as a loud command would be considered a fault. Some riders "click" or "kiss" to their horses as a verbal reinforcing command. I prefer using a word as instruction to the horse.

The use of verbal commands by the rider also keeps the horse from reacting to the show announcer's verbal command as many horses do. My horses may know what the announcer has called for, but they wait until they hear me ask for the new exercise before taking a new action.

If the rider should begin the stopping cues, for example, without having given the horse the verbal command, the horse may experience sudden, confusing pressure of leg and bit. If the rider gives a verbal command first, the horse has time to prepare for the requested action and is not startled by sudden and unexpected pressures.

The timing of the voice command is not critical when the rider asks for the walk, jog, or lope. It is not even critical when the rider asks for a stop from the walk or jog, since the horse always has a hind foot grounded during these gaits. But timing is an important consideration when the rider asks the horse to stop while loping. If the rider requests the action as the horse's head begins its downward motion, then the horse may prepare to stop with the hind feet while both are off the ground for a fraction of a second. The horse can then control his hindquarters and make a solid, square stop, if the rider gives him an opportunity to do so.

4

Cues to Control the Horse

As HORSE and rider advance in their ability to work together as a team, cues will become more subtle, almost imperceptible to any viewer. Mental communication between horse and rider, always followed by a physical response, will soon take over, and the outward signs of cues being given, both verbal commands and physical movement, will seem to disappear.

This state of quiet agreement is most desirable. It comes only when the horse and rider have mutual respect and trust and are in a state of harmony. Patience, understanding, and hours of practice must precede mental communication between the two. Such a state can never be forced. It must be earned and must evolve naturally.

A condition of pure mental telepathy is not achieved, although it would seem to be. What actually occurs is a coinciding of both horse and rider's mental patterns which unconsciously generate physical movement.

For example, if the rider wishes to move forward, his thought to do so motivates a physical reaction. He lifts the reins slightly and unconsciously and unnoticeably tightens his leg muscles. The horse simply moves forward because the desire for such action is understood. Thus, the rider mentally leads the horse.

When an exercise is learned, the rider will initiate the action by thinking about it and reacting in an instinctive physical manner. As the pattern is communicated through the mental and physical actions of the rider, the horse interprets, understands, and assumes control over the completion of the exercise.

To achieve this teamwork, the rider leads the horse until the horse receives the message, interprets it, and then begins to complete the work on his own.

In any fast action, the horse will be the quicker of the partners. The rider, therefore, must begin in a leading position in order to remain in balance with the horse as the horse finishes the action. To lead the horse through an action exercise, the rider uses three cues, always given in sequence, almost simultaneously.

In sequence, the cues of western riding should always be weight shift, legs, and finally hands (reins). The sequence will change only when information prior to action is being communicated.

For example, let's examine how the cues are used when the rider wishes the horse to move out to the right at a walk. When the western horse is at rest, the reins are quite loose, even dropped down on the horse's neck. The rider signals the horse that action is about to begin by gently picking up the reins. With the lifting of the reins, the horse should become alert, but he should not move until the rider indicates the type of work, the direction, and the gait at which the exercise is to be performed. This is done by using the combination of cues.

With a well-schooled, responsive western horse, the rider need only look to the right and apply leg pressure imperceptibly to have the horse move off to the right at the walk.

The finished western horse needs no more instruction than to have the rider think, "I'd like to move to the right at the walk." The rider will then, most often without conscious effort, complete the cues by looking to the right — a movement which shifts the rider's weight to the right and brings the rider's legs against the horse. The sensitive horse understands the weight

In a turn to the right, the rider, by shifting her weight, causes her legs to move into the horse, thereby giving the turn cues.

shift and leg pressure and moves in the direction and at the gait expressed by the rider's cues.

By just looking to the right, the rider has established the correct sequence of cues — the weight shift, then leg pressure, followed by a movement of the reins.

The good western rider never attempts to rein the well-schooled horse into any action. The reining of the western horse always follows the weight-shift and leg cues — cues which exert more control than the rein cue.

There are three basic rein cues for the western horse — the indirect rein, the direct rein, and the indirect rein of opposition.

The principal goal of the western rein cue is to get the horse to seek the center of the reins by moving away from rein pressure. The reins lie along each side of the horse's neck and, when relaxed, do not apply pressure. When no pressure is applied by either rein, the horse is said to be "in the center of the reins."

If the horse finds the center of the reins and if the rider is correctly relinquishing control to the horse once the action has started, the horse will then be in position to complete the exercise on his own.

The only other purposes of rein or bit cues in western riding are to inform the horse of an upcoming action, by telling the horse which head position is required, and to act as a barrier, informing the horse that the rider does not want him to move beyond the present position. The reins are never, never jerked short with the western horse unless disciplinary action is called for.

As mentioned earlier, the rider shortened the reins when mounting, taking a basic direct rein of opposition. Mouth contact was established and the bit acted as a barrier to inform the horse that no movement was desired. But once the rider is mounted, the reins are loosened to the point of dropping them down on the neck. This action tells the horse to remain relaxed and resting. No action is forthcoming.

When the rider is ready for movement, the reins are lifted gently, alerting the horse to impending action. If the rider wishes to move forward at the walk, the reins are left reasonably loose so there is a slight looping of the reins. The bit hangs naturally in the horse's mouth without pressure and the horse's muscles are not shortened in any way. With the reins in this position, the horse has been informed that the rider has selected the walk as the desired gait. When the rider exerts equal pressure gently with both legs, the horse will begin the walking movement in a straight line.

The western horse's body will be extended to its fullest length when the horse is walking, and for this pace, the rider does not want to interfere with that extension of muscle by shortening the reins.

As the horse moves along, the rider may make a decision to turn to the right. In thinking, "I wish to go to the right," the rider looks in the desired direction of travel and this small movement naturally shifts his body weight to the right. With the slight turning of the body including the shoulders, there is a corresponding weight shift to the right, and the rider's legs will fall naturally into the correct cueing position, with the left leg slightly forward and the right leg somewhat back.

At the walk, the exertion of leg pressure is minimal, as is the shifting of the legs forward and back. The principle remains true, however, that the left leg, simply through the twisting movement of the upper body, exerts the greater pressure. The western horse, having been taught to move away from the greater pressure, therefore begins a turn to the right.

The rider's right leg, having moved slightly back toward the horse's flank, exerts a lesser pressure, but still enough to indicate to the horse that a continued driving action with the right hind leg is necessary. This rear driving action allows the horse to step well under himself, which in turn permits lateral flexion of the spine, or a bending to the right.

The western horse will always attempt to move away from pressure and to the rider's weight, keeping that weight centered. The horse increases or decreases his speed of movement relative to the amount of weight shift and leg pressure.

The rider delivers the final bit of information to the horse by slight indirect rein, in this case with the left rein pushed gently against the left side of the horse's neck. The horse will move his head and neck to the right, seeking the newly established center point between the reins.

If done naturally and gently, indirect reining results in an easy response from the horse. Turns to the right or left will not be made sharply, since no braking action is involved. If the

With weight shift to the right, the rider's left leg exerts a stronger pressure, and the horse moves away from it to the right.

rider uses the indirect rein on the horse to make a circle to the left, the horse will make a large circle, always greater in diameter than twice the length of the horse's body.

The second western reining action is the direct rein of opposition. This is used to slow the horse, to initiate or regain a collected position, and to bring the horse behind the bit. The direct rein of opposition is achieved by rolling or moving the reining hand back toward the rider's stomach.

In using the California style of reining, the rider may simply roll the wrist so the little finger points at the stomach. In this manner, the reins, which come up through the hand, are shortened in direct opposition to the horse's direction of travel. If Texas-style reining is being used, the rider will move his entire hand toward his stomach a sufficient distance to apply direct rein opposition to the horse's movement.

As the horse moves forward, the western rider may use the direct rein of opposition to slow the horse. This calls for a "bumping" action in which the rider shortens the rein with a smooth, gentle tug which establishes mouth contact. The bump of the bit should never be punishing, but should be informative, telling the horse to slow his forward movement.

It is essential that the rider never pull steadily on the rein. The rein is shortened, then released immediately. If the rider should fail to release the pressure, the result is the hardening

The direct rein of opposition is pulled gently straight back, then immediately released, cueing the horse to slow the gait.

of the horse's mouth and an eventual refusal to respond to the communication.

When riding the western horse trained to the intermediate level, the rider may be required to use the bumping action of the direct rein of opposition every five to ten strides, as the horse may not have yet learned to hold a steady pace. The advanced horse needs to be bumped infrequently, as he has learned to hold a steady pace over a long period of time.

Generally, the direct rein of opposition is not required when the horse is walking. Most western riders expect a good horse to have a natural, flat-footed walk which covers a lot of ground. But with an inexperienced horse which tends to break from the walk or fails to concentrate satisfactorily on the direction of travel, the rider may use the direct rein of opposition to bump the horse as a disciplinary measure, returning him to the proper gait or getting his attention back on the desired line of travel.

Collecting the horse is simply a matter of moving the horse's natural balance point toward the hindquarters. When the horse is at rest, the natural balance point is just behind and above the horse's elbow and in front of the rider. To collect the horse properly, this balance point must be moved under the rider. This is accomplished by shortening the horse's neck and chest muscles, driving the hindquarters further under the horse and rounding the spinal column through direct flexion.

The western rider uses the direct rein of opposition to collect the horse, but the method differs from bumping. For collection, the rein is slowly and gently shortened, and at the same time, the rider squeezes the horse gently with both legs. By using equal, mild leg pressure, the rider is telling the horse to move forward. Since all action originates with the hindquarters, the hindquarters move first and are placed further under the horse. The horse is said to be "pushed" to the bit, while the direct rein of opposition keeps the horse from moving forward out of his present position. When the hindquarters can no longer move forward, direct flexion of the spine takes place and, finally, the horse shortens his chest and neck muscles, flexes at the poll, relaxes the jaw, and brings the head into the vertical position.

When the horse is pushed to the bit, he will drop his head and neck somewhat to relieve any direct rein-of-opposition pressure which he feels through the bit. He is then in a collected position and ready for the next action.

If the rider has only shortened the reins a little, the horse will be able to walk in a collected manner. But if the rein has been shortened to a greater degree, the horse will recognize that a greater shortening of his body is required if he is to be free of bit pressure. He relieves this pressure by moving forward at the jog, which is a more elevated gait than the walk. When he is jogging, the horse's body is rounded and therefore shortened, allowing the horse to feel bit contact but avoid bit pressure.

If the reins are shortened still further, the horse will be required to shorten his body even more, rounding it to a greater degree. The horse can do this by changing his gait from the walk or jog to the lope, the most elevated stride of the western horse.

The horse must also be collected in order to back properly. The direct rein of opposition is used to move the horse's natural balance from the forehand to the hindquarters.

The rider must remember that all direct rein-of-opposition cues are given in combination with leg-pressure cues. The horse must be "pushed" to the bit by use of the legs.

The direct rein of opposition is also used to remind the horse to remain somewhat behind the bit, the basic difference between the way a classically trained horse travels and the way the western horse travels. Being "on the bit" means there is slight mouth contact through the reins to the rider's hands. The classically trained horse is always on the bit.

The western horse which has been trained to an advanced level carries himself as if he were on the bit, but he is not. The good western rider always makes sure there is a little slack in

Off the bit.

On the bit.

the reins once the horse's head has been positioned properly. The western horse is pushed to the bit, which tells the horse that particular position is the desired position for the upcoming exercise. Then the rider loosens the rein, expecting the horse not to change his body position, but to maintain it and perform the exercise on his own.

If the horse forgets or loses his concentration, the western rider uses the direct rein of opposition in a bumping action to remind the horse to get back behind the bit, but the contact is brief.

The direct rein of opposition should never be used in a punishing manner by jerking on the rein, and the good rider is careful never to do so, unless the punishment is intended as discipline for disobedience. After bumping with the direct rein of opposition, pressure is released immediately, just as it is when the direct rein of opposition is used to change the horse's natural balance point by shortening his body.

The indirect rein of opposition is the most difficult and complicated of the three basic western riding rein actions. It must both brake the forward movement and turn the horse at the same time. The reins must be pulled back (opposition) and laid against the horse's neck (indirect), signaling a halt and a turn.

Correct placement for the indirect rein of opposition in a rollback to the right, for example, requires the rider to pull the reins back toward the right hip of both himself and the horse. This puts the left rein against the horse's neck on the left side, just in front of the withers, exerting both indirect and opposition pressures.

The rider must be extremely careful that the indirect rein of opposition is not too forceful. Too much pressure will both jerk the horse's head to the left, since the rein is being shortened more on that side, and elevate the forehand, since the horse's forward movement is being blocked by a fixed bit position. To tilt the horse's head away from the direction of travel is incorrect, as is elevating the forehand. The forehand should remain

In the rollback, the rider must shift her weight both to the horse's hindquarters, to drive the horse, and into the direction of turn.

low, and the horse moves away from the indirect rein pressure.

The opposition rein pressure must be strong enough to brake the right hind foot, but not so strong as to lift the forehand.

If the rider wants to do a rollback, he begins communication with the horse by turning his upper body in the direction of travel desired. This turning shifts the rider's weight and begins the positioning of the rider's legs. The rider completes his instructions to the horse by use of the indirect rein of opposition. This conveys to the horse the message that braking the hindquarters is required, as is turning to seek a new center point between the reins.

If the rider wishes to roll back to the right, he turns the upper body to the right and begins to look back in the expected direction of travel. The rider's left leg moves forward slightly, signaling to the horse that a forehand movement away from leg pressure is required. The right leg moves back toward the flank, indicating that a continuing driving action is necessary. The rider moves his hand toward his own right hip, bringing the left (indirect) rein across the horse's neck to apply indirect pressure while also applying opposition pressure to forward movement.

The reining movement causes the bit to create a barrier to further movement, thereby requesting a braking action by the hindquarters. The indirect rein pressure tells the horse to seek a new center point between the reins, which is now somewhere off to the right.

Once the horse has come around far enough to the right to find the center point between the reins, he will discover there is no longer any indirect rein-of-opposition pressure. The relief from all pressure is both the horse's reward for having responded correctly and his cue to relax, yet remain alert for the next series of cues.

How the horse responds to any of the three rein positions depends on his gait at the time. If the horse is walking, a quick response to the rider's weight and leg shifts is not required, since both rider movements would only be slight. On the other hand, if the horse is loping, he will respond more readily to the cues since they will have a greater influence over his natural balance.

In all reining action, the horse's head remains low and he stays relaxed only if the rider cues him gently. The use of excessive force or jerking on the reins causes the horse much discomfort, and he will show his displeasure by tossing his head or, even worse, resisting the rein pressure and fighting the weight and leg cues.

Although the western rider is usually pictured as riding with the reins held in one hand, it is not always a wise practice. Only the very best western riders on well-schooled horses will be able to accomplish all exercises without applying unnecessary rein pressure.

It is a good idea for the novice or intermediate western rider to ride frequently holding a rein in each hand. This practice assists the horse in learning to seek the center of reins and helps him avoid the problem of overflexing on the side on which the rider naturally carries the reins.

If the rider who carries his reins in his left hand is not very careful, or if the horse is not well schooled, there will be a tendency on the part of the rider to apply pressure unconsciously to the right side of the bit. The horse gives to this pressure and flexes to the right. Eventually, the horse will get in the habit of always being a little flexed to the right.

The very best western horses have learned to seek the center of the reins and to remain behind the bit. They are ridden by riders wise enough never to apply unwanted or unconscious rein pressure.

5

Weight-Shift Cues

ONCE the western rider understands the basic leg and rein aids used to request the horse to walk, jog, lope, and stop while moving in a straight line, he can begin to learn the weight-shift cues needed to make turns.

Instructors of the classic style of equitation always advise the rider not to twist the upper body or to lean into a turn. Their goal is to have the rider keep the upper body erect at all times, his weight in the center of the horse's back.

This is not the case with the western-trained horse and rider. A classically trained horse is never left free to control the completion of an exercise, nor is he asked to work with speed, as is the western horse. The western horse is given freedom to finish the exercise and he is expected to do it quickly, with grace and balance. The western rider must indicate what is expected of the horse by providing an understandable cue, then he must assist the horse by leading him into the exercise at the same time he is releasing control to the horse.

By twisting the upper body and/or leaning into the desired direction of travel in making turns, the rider both leads the horse and positions himself to be in balance with the horse when the horse moves at his own speed to complete the request.

In western riding, no rider can remain seated in the center of the horse's back, give the cues for a spin, and then expect to stay in balance with the responsive, well-trained, reining horse. The horse will simply be too fast for the rider's reaction. The rider is left behind the horse and immediately becomes a hindrance to the horse in his effort to complete the exercise correctly.

The rider therefore must learn how to twist his body and lean in the direction of travel by first learning the appropriate weight-shift cues. He must learn the cues for slow, basic turns and suppling exercises before he can go on to more advanced riding patterns.

The western horse has been taught to move away from pressure and toward a shift in the rider's weight. By moving toward the weight shift, the horse brings himself and his rider back into balance because he moves under the weight in an effort to support the weight.

As we have already established, all action originates in the horse's hindquarters, and all rider requests for action are initiated by leg-pressure cues. The cue should be a "pressing" one rather than a kicking motion. The horse should feel the pressure of this cue first from the calf of the rider's leg. If this pressure is not sufficient to evoke the expected response from the horse, the rider may then apply greater pressure by using more of the lower leg. The maximum pressure results from use of the heel.

In moving the leg back or forward to apply a pressure cue in the appropriate spot, the rider must be careful that the knees do not move away from the saddle. To avoid this error, the rider must let his toes move out toward a right angle as far as necessary. Many riders make the mistake of trying to keep their toes parallel to the horse's sides while applying pressure cues with their legs. It simply cannot be done, because if the toes stay parallel, the knees have a tendency to leave the saddle, and the rider may lose his seat or find that his upper body sways undesirably.

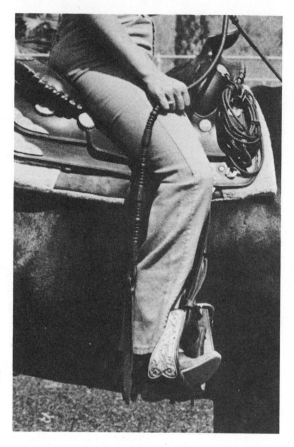

When cueing the
horse with a pressing
heel to initiate action,
the rider should allow
the toe to turn out
rather than allowing
the heel to rise.

Of course, it is correct to keep the toes almost parallel to the
horse's sides when the rider's legs are at rest, but it is equally
right to let the toe angle out when the rider gives a pressure
cue. By turning the toes out, the rider can keep his knees
snugly against the saddle, maintain a secure seat, and keep his
heels down. If the knees come away from the saddle, the heels
are automatically brought up; these actions are incorrect.

The first cue then for a simple turn to the left is right leg
pressure, applied by the calf of the leg, and a slight turn to the
left by the rider's upper body. These actions are immediately
followed by a reining action in which indirect rein pressure is
applied gently to the right side of the horse's neck.

If the horse is already moving satisfactorily at the walk, then the rider has only the lightest leg contact with the horse's sides. This contact is not the result of any squeezing action by the legs, but is the natural contact experienced when the rider is well seated and relaxed. The legs are at rest, and therefore the rider's toes naturally are positioned parallel to the horse's body.

In turning the shoulders and hips slightly to the left, the rider has automatically shifted a small portion of his body weight to the horse's left side. At the same time, the change in body position alone has brought the rider's right leg into a position where it presses gently into the horse's right side. The natural tendency of the rider's toe then is to turn out, angling away from the horse's body. This action is correct, and if done unconsciously, the heel remains down and the rider can cue at the

In shifting the upper body and weight for a turn, the rider's leg moves naturally into the correct position for a leg-pressure cue.

In a left turn, the body shift moves the rider's right leg forward, while the left leg moves slightly back; the heel stays down and the toe moves out.

proper location (near the girth) to indicate to the horse there is a desire for forehand movement to the left, away from the side pressure on the right.

Without trying to stop any of the body movement which has been initiated naturally, the rider will discover his left leg drops back somewhat toward the horse's flank, and if all natural body movement is allowed to continue, the inclination of the toe of the left foot will be to turn out, thus keeping the heel down. The left leg will also fall naturally into the proper cue position to indicate to the horse that continued driving action with the left hind leg is desired.

When the rider turns his upper body to the left, it is also natural for him to look to the left and for his left hand to move to the left, creating a spontaneous indirect rein pressure on the right side of the horse's neck.

So, we can see that the simple desire to turn to the left has resulted in the rider's automatically giving all the cues necessary to inform the horse that a left turn is desired. If the responses to the thought occur naturally, rather than being forced, all cues will be placed perfectly. The rider will find there is never a need to force cues or strain to reach the proper cue positions.

Force, or unnecessary effort, is usually the result of the novice rider's attempting to hold back natural movement or overcue the horse to compensate for lack of confidence in the horse's ability to respond.

Natural western riding does not require the rider to force the horse into position. If the horse has been well schooled and understands the request, he will assume the correct position naturally. Correspondingly, excessive weight shifts are never necessary.

After the horse has moved to the left or right to the degree desired by the rider, the cues for the turn are discontinued, and the horse will then begin straight movement, content in the knowledge there is no leg pressure to move away from, weight shift to move to, or center of the reins to seek.

The rider twists body to right for right offset, allowing right leg to hold hindquarters, while left leg pushes forehand to right.

The rider can make circles by giving the exact same cues used for a left or right turn, except that the cues are held until the horse has completed a single circle or several circles. In making circles with a western horse, the rider should remember not to turn the horse in a distance shorter than the length of the horse. This holds true with a half-turn to the left or right.

The offset is a turning exercise in which the rider holds the horse's hindquarters stationary while moving the forehand 90 degrees or 180 degrees to the right or left. This exercise is started when the horse is standing still and is accomplished by weight shifts, very slight changes in leg position, and gentle reining.

If the offset is done properly, the horse will move the inside hind foot (the right foot if the offset is to the right; the left foot if the offset is to the left) a few inches forward in order to establish that foot as the pivot foot and better to support his own and the rider's weight. The horse uses his other three legs to push his body around the pivot foot.

The offset is started by the rider's shifting his weight to the rear and in the direction of desired travel. If the rider wishes a quarter-turn to the right, he shifts his weight back toward and onto the horse's right hind foot. The rider also turns his upper body a little to the right. This movement drops the rider's right leg slightly back toward the horse's flank. The new leg pressure tells the horse to move the right hind foot forward. At the same time, the weight shift forces the horse to ground his right foot quickly since it is needed as the major support. With the twisting of the upper body, the rider's left leg moves a little forward. However, no pressure is required from this leg.

The rider applies an indirect left rein pressure, which tells the horse to move away and seek the center of the reins.

The horse will lift the forehand and swing his body smoothly to the right as long as the rider's cues are not too forceful. The offset exercise loses its smoothness when the rider's cues are too rough and severe.

If the rider wants a quarter-turn, then he barely twists his upper body. If a half-turn is desired, the rider must turn the upper body to a greater degree.

As the horse responds to the weight, leg, and rein cues, the rider will determine the degree of the offset by making sure his weight will be centered on the horse when the horse reaches the 90-degree point. If the rider wants a half-circle offset of 180 degrees, then he must continue his own weight-shift and rein cues until the horse reaches the desired point, after which time the rider's weight is again centered.

The horse stops the offset exercise the moment he has moved under the rider's weight and has reestablished the rider in a resting position.

When rocking the horse as a practice exercise for offsets, the rider must remember to make the cues gentle and rhythmic. If the cues are not smooth and light, the horse will respond by bouncing erratically.

Normally the offset is considered a fast exercise in which the horse lifts the forehand and swings it in one motion of approximately 90 degrees. As with all western riding exercises, however, the rider's responsibility is to make the cues as gentle and subtle as possible while making sure they are completely understood by the horse. The rider must never attempt to force speed. Speed on the part of the rider is not desirable and is not his responsibility.

The horse is an equal member of the partnership. While the request for performance is controlled by the rider, the speed of the performance, when required, is determined by the horse and his ability to fulfill the request with grace and balance.

Speed, grace, and balance develop as the horse and rider learn to work as a single unit. The rider initiates and the horse completes.

The greatest mistake a western rider can make is to believe he can force the horse into a better position than one the horse will assume naturally. If it is ever necessary for the rider to control the ultimate positioning of the western-trained horse, one of two failures has occurred. The horse has not been informed properly and educated as to what is required, or the horse simply does not have the natural physical ability to perform at the level desired. In most cases, the training is at fault. But in some cases, the horse cannot attain the level of performance sought because of his disposition, temperament, or conformation. Western-trained horses which become champions do so because they have superior ability. No amount of training can create that ability. It is the rider's responsibility to help the horse reach his potential, whatever that may be, and never attempt to push the horse beyond his physical capabilities.

6

Stopping and Backing

THE PHILOSOPHY of natural western riding is probably never more visibly violated than when the egocentric rider becomes a dictator and tries to overpower his horse when stopping and backing. There is no need for force, yet it is frequently employed.

Stopping and backing are the same as all other exercises performed by horse and rider. They require teamwork if beauty and balance are to be the result. The rider asks for the stop, cues the horse with a communicative aid, then, upon feeling the horse's response, relinquishes control so the horse can finish the exercise on his own, as he can do only when given freedom. Teamwork, without force, is also the rule for backing.

Good western riding is dependent upon cues which are not harsh or severe. But too often when the novice western rider wishes to stop his horse or to back him, gentleness is forgotten and the power play begins. The novice rider attempts to jerk the horse to a stop with the reins. This hurts the horse and can damage his mouth. Similarly, when the novice rider wants to back his horse, he invariably pulls straight back on the reins, applying a constant pressure which is again painful. He forgets the cardinal rule that any degree of pressure must be followed by immediate relief from that pressure.

In stopping and backing a horse, remember that a shift in

the rider's weight and pressure from his legs are the principal cues, and that the reining (hand) cues always follow the first two and are subordinate to them.

The western rider must learn the timing and proper feel of a good stop. It takes practice, practice, and more practice because a number of cues must be employed in the correct sequence.

The horse's anatomy is designed for speed and running long distances, not for quick, hard stops. Of course, the horse is capable of making such stops, but even when he is at play and there is no rider on his back, he does so infrequently. When he is carrying a rider, his hard stops are often made with a great deal of reluctance.

The horse's rear legs are principally driving units rather than well-engineered stopping devices. The rear foot is smaller than the front foot, and its design is best for a digging-in type of traction rather than for sliding while remaining on top of the ground. The fetlocks are strong and flexible but are not of the best design to lock and hold the weight of both horse and rider for relatively long periods of time. The hocks are susceptible to injury from strain, and of course they are under severe stress during a quick, hard sliding stop.

Nevertheless, we expect the western horse to stop quickly. (Doesn't every movie cowboy jerk his horse to a quick, hard stop in front of every hitching rail?) In the show ring, the western horse is expected to run out with speed and perform the spectacular, but difficult, slide stop. These expectations make it incumbent upon the rider to give cues correctly so the stopping exercise remains as safe and easy for the horse as possible. There is also the element of danger to both horse and rider with any fast, hard exercise. However, if the rider avoids any attempt to overpower the horse and force compliance, the danger will be lessened, since the horse can then work to his natural ability.

Since slide stops cause tremendous stress on the horse, western stock horses have a tendency to "burn out" quickly. It is the wise rider who saves the slide stop for the show ring and practices on form and position, working the horse at the walk, jog, and slow lope. Once the horse knows how to stop, he will slide-stop. There is no reason to break the horse down by asking for continual, unnecessary strain.

The first cue in stopping a horse is a command to stop. I use a verbal command, "Ho," because I believe the horse likes to perform and he appreciates being told in a nice way that something is expected of him. However, a substitute cue can be used, such as touching the horse's neck just in front of the saddle horn. But the rider must always use the same introductory cue with every stop, for it is this cue which informs the horse of the difficult work ahead.

A rider may well find that at slow speed the horse can be stopped without undue pain or punishment even when the primary cue is not given. It is knowledge of the correct timing which permits a good stop without the introductory cue. However, once the horse has advanced to the runout and slide stop, the timing element has been lost. The horse will be moving with such great speed that it is impossible for the rider to judge with sufficient accuracy the correct instant to begin the second cue.

The rider must employ the introductory cue — in our example, the verbal command — and wait until he feels the horse react. It takes a moment for the horse to receive the message, digest it, send the correct instructions to the muscles, and then have the muscles react correctly to produce the requested action. When the horse understands the introductory cue, he'll begin to react, and the horse's reaction should then draw forth assistance from the rider.

At the walk, the horse moves in a four-beat gait. At no time does he have both hind feet off the ground, so when the rider gives the initiating cue, "Ho," the horse begins to stop, and the rider then employs the second cue of the sequence, which is equal pressure with both legs. The rider's leg pressure encourages a continued driving action by the horse's hind legs, making sure the horse will have his hind feet well under him when he has completed the stop.

As the rider begins his leg-pressure cue, he must also tighten his stomach muscles, dropping the pelvis back and down and locking his seat in the saddle. This muscle tightening also causes the rider's upper body to incline forward. This is the most desirable position for a rider during a slide stop.

The rider must never throw himself back in the saddle to stop. It puts him out of position and invariably makes him jerk on the reins. Leaning back to force a hard stop may seem to be a natural tendency, but it is the worst mistake a rider can make during a stop.

However, if the rider will always use the third cue, tightening his stomach muscles, he will find that it is impossible for him to lean back and that he is automatically slanting somewhat forward — the correct position.

The fourth cue in stopping a horse involves use of the reins. As the stomach muscles are tightened, the rider moves his reining hand back toward his stomach until the reins have been shortened enough to establish mouth contact with the horse. The hand is then held steady, and the horse begins to bend his spine in direct flexion to avoid going past the bit, which now acts as a barrier.

At all costs, the rider must avoid pulling the bit back in the horse's mouth. The rider's fixed hand simply holds the bit in position and the horse's forward motion carries the horse to the bit.

As the horse reaches his maximum flexion, the rider must release the bit barrier by returning his hand to its natural position over the saddle horn, thereby avoiding unnecessary pressure on the horse's mouth. The rider must understand that it is his responsibility to eliminate excessive pressure on the horse's mouth by never letting the horse's forward movement push the

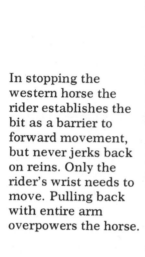

In stopping the western horse the rider establishes the bit as a barrier to forward movement, but never jerks back on reins. Only the rider's wrist needs to move. Pulling back with entire arm overpowers the horse.

horse beyond the point of light mouth contact with the bit.

The horse has little forward motion at the walk and will have little direct spinal flexion when stopping. Therefore, the horse can compensate for his impulsion by arching his neck and flexing at the poll. Seldom is the horse's mouth damaged when he is being stopped from a walk.

The jog produces greater forward movement, and a stop from this gait requires more concentration and feel from the rider. At the lope, the horse has enough forward motion that his maximum direct spinal flexion cannot keep him behind the bit barrier during the stop. For this reason, it is at the lope that the rider must be sure the bit barrier is removed the instant after mouth contact has been established.

The rider must also be aware of how changes of gait affect the horse's hind feet during the stop. Since the horse never has both hind feet off the ground while he is walking, there cannot be a stop with the rear feet perfectly squared at this gait. The same is true at the jog, since one rear foot is always grounded when the introductory cue for stopping is given.

At the lope, however, there is a brief moment when both hind feet are off the ground. And with both hind feet off the ground, the horse can bring his hind feet together to make a solid, squared stop.

The rider need not concern himself with the movement of the horse's feet at the walk and jog, since at these gaits the responsive western horse will stop as soon as the introductory cue is given, and almost before the rider can complete the remaining three cues — leg pressure, weight shift, and mouth contact with the bit.

When the horse is loping, however, the rider must give the first cue just prior to the moment when the horse has both hind feet off the ground. This occurs just as the leading forefoot is striking the ground. As the horse moves into this position, with the leading forefoot coming down, the horse's head will also be dropping, since he is moving into his greatest extension during this phase of the gait. It is at this moment — when the horse's head begins to drop — that the rider gives the verbal command, "Ho."

There is enough time following this cue for the horse to interpret the message and prepare himself for the stop. The rider then assists the horse with leg pressure, weight shift (by tightening the stomach muscles), and rein cue (to establish mouth contact).

The final action by the rider is the immediate release of the reins after mouth contact has been established.

If all cues are given properly and in sequence, the horse will stop from the lope squarely on both hind feet. His head will remain relatively low, and his front feet will continue in a

The rider gives verbal command "Ho" as leading foreleg strikes the ground and hindfeet are about to leave the ground.

walking action until his forward impulsion has been dissipated.

During the rundown and slide stop in the show ring, some western riders like to see both front feet come off the ground and be extended stiffly in front of the horse as he slides. As spectacular as this might be to see, it is, in my opinion, incorrect. I would prefer to have the horse's front feet continue the walking action, striking the ground in sequence as the horse slides. In doing so, the front feet give the horse the support he needs for balance and also make it possible for him to turn even though he has not come to a complete stop.

The hard stop is supposedly employed only when the rider finds it imperative to change direction in a hurry (as when following a calf which has turned back). But if the horse's front feet are completely off the ground during the entire slide stop, the horse is in no position to reverse his direction.

When the horse stops hard and fast, it is natural for him to

When the horse is walking with the front feet, and sliding with both hind feet, then he is stopping properly.

In stopping hard, the horse naturally lifts his head and neck. The rider should have a slack rein after bit barrier is established.

lift his head and neck as a means of keeping his balance. This is most desirable. However, if the horse throws his head wildly, opens his mouth, or tucks his head to his chest, the rider is at fault because he did not relinquish control of the final phase of the exercise to the horse. These three "fault" signs are all caused by the rider's failing to release the reins immediately, discontinuing mouth contact. Too many times these faults are the result of the rider using the reins to keep his own balance. But if the rider will tighten his stomach muscles and squeeze with his legs, there should be no need to use the reins for balance since the rider will be locked down in the saddle.

Once the rider has learned and practiced the cues needed to stop his horse successfully, he can go on to learning the correct body position and aids needed to back the horse.

The good western rider never pulls the horse back with the reins when he wants the horse to back. If he does this, the horse will either open his mouth to escape the pain of unnecessary bit pressure, tuck his head to his chest, or throw his head in the air to force the rider to extend the reins.

Proper backing of the western horse is accomplished, again, by giving the proper sequence of cues. These are shortening the reins, shifting the rider's weight, and application of leg pressure. None of these cues ever employs force to achieve the wanted result.

To back the horse, the rider must first shorten the reins gently and slowly until mouth contact has been established. Once established, the rider continues to shorten the reins without jerking them until the horse shifts his own weight to his rear legs. The horse will shift his weight if he is asked to do so in a courteous manner. If the reins are not shortened cautiously, the horse will rebel by moving his head out of position in an effort to avoid unnecessary bit pressure.

Once the horse has shifted his weight to the rear legs, light contact with the mouth should be maintained by the rider's fixed hand. The fixed hand establishes the bit as a barrier to forward movement by the horse.

In backing, the rider shortens the reins gently until the horse
shifts his weight to hindquarters, then the rider applies leg aids.

The rider must now shift his weight from the horse's back to
the horse's withers. This is done by transferring his weight so
it is carried by his feet and the stirrups. It is not necessary for
the rider to stand in the stirrups; a slight weight shift from the
saddle seat to the stirrups is sufficient. This weight transfer
frees the horse's spine, allowing the horse to bend the spine
upward easily in direct flexion.

With the weight shift accomplished, the rider can then ask
for movement from the horse. This is done by using both legs
to squeeze with equal pressure. The horse will move backward
until the rider's leg pressure is discontinued, signaling the
horse that no further movement is required.

With the horse's weight shifted to hindquarters, the horse jogs backward without lifting his head. The rider controls speed with leg aids.

If the rider stops the leg pressure but holds the reins in the shortened position, the horse will continue to keep his weight on his rear legs. With his weight on his rear legs, the horse is ready to move backward again with the renewal of leg pressure by the rider.

If the rider should change the rein position, removing the barrier to forward motion, but continue the leg pressure, the horse will respond immediately to the continued leg pressure by moving forward.

If both rider cues stop and the rider returns his weight to the saddle seat, the horse will stop all movement immediately and remain at rest.

The rider uses both leg and rein cues to control the direction of the horse's backward movement. For example, to move the hindquarters to the right, the rider applies increased left leg pressure back toward the horse's flank. The horse will move his hindquarters away from the increase in pressure while continuing to back.

If the rider wishes the forehand to swing to the left, he need only apply indirect rein pressure to the right side of the horse's neck. Again, the horse will move away from the pressure while continuing to respond to the rider's leg pressures which are calling for backward movement.

To negotiate obstacles while backing, it is often necessary for the rider to use a complex set of compensating cues to match the circumstances of the moment. It may be necessary for the rider to stop the horse (discontinue leg pressure), then move the hindquarters to the right while holding the forehand (left leg pressure back toward the flank; right leg pressure at the girth).

Such exercises call for a combination of skills in both horse and rider. The rider must give the correct cues at the proper time and the horse must learn how to respond to the cues. Practice, done quietly and consistently, results in the teamwork needed.

Well-executed stops and backing can never be forced by the rider. The serious western rider will always try to strengthen the partnership by never overpowering the horse or failing to relinquish control at the proper time.

7

Bending and Suppling Exercises

CONTROL of the initiating action for any exercise is the responsibility of the rider, who asks the horse for a particular exercise by giving the proper cues and then, upon recognizing the horse's understanding, relinquishes control, allowing the horse to complete the exercise.

It is this freedom given by the rider which makes possible the quick, smooth, natural action of the western-trained horse. If the rider attempts to control the entire action, the horse is hampered. If the rider fails to present his request adequately in the form of understandable cues, then the horse cannot be blamed for failing to complete the action confidently.

This technique of requesting action and then relinquishing control applies to such exercises as the shoulder-in, the travers, renvers, and rollback, as well as the pivot on the forehand or hindquarters. Mastery of these exercises indicates the rider is progressing well and learning to share the responsibilities of performance with his partner.

The shoulder-in, the travers, and the renvers are demonstrations of the rider's ability to control the positioning of the forehand and the hindquarters at the same time. These exercises are accomplished most easily if the rider holds the reins in two hands. However, with practice and a horse which is advanced in training, the exercises may be done with the rider holding the reins in one hand.

To perform "shoulder-in," the rider must hold the horse's hindquarters with his inside leg while moving the forehand with his outside leg.

The terms "in" and "out" always refer to the center of any circle. If the horse is moving to the left to any degree, then the center of the circle is to the left. The travers, therefore, requires the haunches to be moved to the left, while the renvers requires the haunches to be moved to the right. In an arena, the center of the arena is always "in" and the rail is always "out."

A shoulder-in exercise requires the horse to move the forehand one hoof-width to the inside of the circle. The horse's head and neck should bend just a little toward the center of the circle. The hindquarters, however, must track in a straight line.

If the horse is moving properly in the shoulder-in exercise, a person standing behind the horse will see a definite three-track pattern. For example, in moving to the left, the horse's left forefoot, the foot closest to the center of the circle, will make the first track. The horse's left hind and right fore will track on the same line, and the horse's right hind will track alone, farthest from the center of the circle.

To position the horse for the shoulder-in, the rider must maintain his weight in the middle of the horse, his spine being directly in line with that of the horse. The rider's left leg will drop back toward the horse's flank to hold the hindquarters straight. The rider's right leg must move slightly forward and press the horse at the girth to push the forehand over the width of one hoof. The rider must rein the horse a little to the left, asking the horse to bend his neck in toward the center of the circle.

When first practicing the shoulder-in, the rider will find there is often a tendency to exert too much leg or rein pressure in an attempt to force the horse to move into position. Generally, the horse will respond to this by starting to circle instead of continuing in a straight line. Sometimes the horse will let his hindquarters swing out, away from the rider's inside leg pressure. The rider may find it necessary to make any number of compensating cue adjustments to keep the horse in the three-track position.

If the horse begins to circle, the rider will have to soften the rein cue and move the inside leg cue forward to retard the circling action of the horse's forehand. If the hindquarters should swing away from the inside leg pressure instead of being held by it, the rider will have to correct the horse's position by moving the outside leg cue back toward the horse's flank.

During the learning period, the rider may be required to continue the compensating cues for some time until the horse both understands the exercise and is physically able to perform it properly. It must be kept in mind that the shoulder-in, the travers, and the renvers require the horse to arch his spine. This flexion of the spinal column is difficult to hold for a horse that is not conditioned.

However, when the horse is physically able to do the exercise and understands what is being asked, it is the same lateral spinal flexion which tells the rider the performance is correct. The rider will be able to feel the horse's spine arch as the flexion twists the rider's lower body to a slight degree.

If the rider is on an unresponsive horse, he may find it necessary to bump the horse with his heels to bring the horse into position. This must be done carefully or the horse will change gait immediately, become frightened, or simply circle. For this reason, it is incumbent upon the rider to keep the cues as gentle as possible.

The rider should always begin every request with the lightest possible cue, increasing the pressure of the cue until there is a response. Each time an exercise is requested, the rider begins with the minimal cue, following it with a little more severe one, and then a more aggressive cue until the horse makes an attempt to perform correctly. As both members of the team gain a greater understanding of their respective responsibilities, the cues will become more subtle.

The travers (haunches-in) is accomplished by the rider maintaining his weight in the middle of the horse, cueing with the outside leg back toward the flank, bringing the inside leg forward toward the girth to hold the forehand straight, and applying light direct rein of opposition to fix the bit so the horse does not bend his neck.

When viewing the travers from the rear, the observer should see the horse's hindquarters move one hoof-width toward the inside of the circle. In moving to the left, the horse's left hind foot will track alone closest to the center of the circle. The right hind foot and the left forefoot track together, and the right forefoot tracks alone, farthest from the center of the circle.

The rider will experience the same exaggerated reaction from the novice horse, and again, he must adjust the cues to

"Haunches-in" requires the horse to hold neck and head straight while the hindquarters move one hoof-width to the inside of the circle.

compensate for the horse's inexperience. If the forehand gets out of position, the rider must change one or the other of his leg cues to bring the forehand back to the center. If the hindquarters fail to move over the prescribed one hoof-width, the rider may have to bump the hindquarters over by application of harder heel pressure.

The renvers (haunches-out) is simply the reverse of the travers, and the rider's leg cues will be just the opposite of the travers cues when the horse is moving in the same direction.

Once he has learned to give the proper cues, then feel the horse respond correctly, the rider will be able to exert independent control over the horse's forehand and hindquarters at will. Of course, the horse's body must be in the proper position, but

Renvers and travers exercises help the western rider to supple the horse and gain independent control over hindquarters and forehand. The horse performs renvers, haunches-out.

once the horse learns what is required of him, he'll position himself naturally to work the exercise. However, the horse can't distinguish between one exercise and another unless the rider cues the horse properly so the animal can get his body in the correct position.

The rollback, another suppling exercise, is one which requires continuous movement by the horse, making it necessary for the rider to provide an introductory cue, followed by immediate freedom.

When rolling back, the horse begins the exercise as he would begin a stop. Then the horse steps forward with the inside hind foot and rolls his body back over that foot so he is facing in the opposite direction. When the horse comes out of the rollback at

The rider initiates the rollback by shifting her weight and changing leg-pressure cues. The horse completes the exercise on his own. *Above, right:* Once initiated, the rider allows the horse to finish the exercise. The rider looks where she wants to go, and waits for the horse to complete work. *Bottom:* When the rider wants the horse to "explode" out of the turn, she must lead the horse into the "burst of power" by new body positioning.

the lope, he should be on the lead opposite that which began the exercise. A horse can also do a rollback from the walk or jog, in which case he should continue the same gait when his direction has been reversed.

To accomplish a rollback, the rider must begin by pushing the horse to the bit, which is then held in a fixed position. The rider squeezes with both legs, tightens his stomach muscles, and shifts his weight a little back and to the inside of the circle. The rider does not pull back on the reins, but instead shortens them a little and fixes his hand.

As the horse begins the stop, the rider exerts stronger inside leg pressure, driving the inside hind leg forward. At the same time, the rider must change his outside leg cue to move the forehand around and over the horse's inside pivot foot. To move the outside leg forward, the rider must turn his body to the inside and shift his weight to the inside and slightly back. The reining cue is a light one and follows the leg and weight-shift directional cues. The reining cue must not have any direct opposition pressure, but must be an indirect pressure entirely. The horse will move away from this pressure as he seeks the newly positioned center of the reins.

The horse will recognize the cues and come around, reversing his direction and repositioning his body under the rider's weight. Both horse and rider will be in balance when the horse has completed the 180-degree turn.

As soon as he recognizes that the horse has understood the introductory cues and is positioned to complete the rollback satisfactorily, the rider must release all cues, providing the horse with the freedom he needs to finish the exercise. If the rider has reacted properly, he will be inactive, applying no cue pressures when the exercise is finished. If the rider fails to stop any of his cues, the horse will continue to respond and, in so doing, will be adding some kind of unwanted movement to the exercise. This is not the horse's fault; it is the result of the rider's error in failing to give the horse the freedom he needs.

When the horse has completely reversed his direction, the rider will apply the correct set of cues to reestablish the same gait which preceded the rollback. If the horse was jogging, the rider should immediately apply equal leg pressure to reestablish the jog.

If the rider wants the horse to come out of a rollback from the lope on the right lead, he should lope the horse in the opposite direction on the left lead, provided that the rollback is to be made away from the center of the circle. When the rider cues the horse to roll back to the left, the rider's left leg-pressure cue is back toward the flank, driving the left hind foot well under the horse. As the horse comes out of the rollback, the rider should not be applying any cues, for if the rider has unwisely continued his left leg pressure back toward the flank, the horse will react properly by continuing on the right lead. This is the incorrect lead in relationship to the center of the former circle. On the other hand, if the rider has discontinued all cues, letting the horse finish the exercise in complete freedom, the horse will respond correctly to an entirely new left-lead introductory cue.

Between the completion of one exercise and the beginning of another, the rider should pause before asking for the new exercise. This brief respite is all the horse needs to understand that one exercise has been finished and that a new one may be forthcoming.

Rider cues for the pivot on the hindquarters are often determined by the horse's conformation and natural ability. Some horses have strong hindquarter muscles and can establish and hold a rear pivot foot easily. Others have a difficult time establishing the pivot foot and holding it throughout a 360-degree pivot.

If the horse has strong hindquarters and the rider wishes to pivot to the left, then the rider begins the exercise with a weight shift to the left and to the rear. By shifting the weight to this position, the rider has forced the horse's left rear foot to bear more weight than the other feet, inhibiting its freedom to move.

The rider then applies left leg pressure back toward the flank, moving the horse's left hind foot forward in a short stride. Continued left leg pressure then holds the left hind foot forward.

Right leg pressure toward the girth (to move the forehand to the left) is then applied by the rider, as is light, indirect right rein pressure. The horse should move slowly to the left, seeking the new center of the reins and avoiding the light right leg pressure. The rider may find it necessary to apply some direct rein of opposition if the horse attempts to move forward. The rider will have to adjust his cues if he finds the horse is weak in his hindquarters and wants to swing his hindquarters to the right to avoid both the rider's left leg pressure and the necessary slight spinal arch.

Instead of applying continuous left leg pressure to drive the horse's left hind foot forward, the rider will apply left leg pressure, then immediately release it. Such a cue gets the horse to move the left hind foot forward in a straight line. Discontinuing the pressure keeps the horse from moving the hindquarters off to the right.

Instead of applying right leg pressure at the girth to move the forehand to the left, the rider applies right leg pressure back toward the flank to keep the hindquarters in position.

With this set of leg cues, the rider must rely to a greater extent on the indirect rein cue to move the forehand to the left.

The rider should keep his body weight in the center of the horse if the horse has a tendency to swing the hindquarters in the direction opposite to the intended pivot. The centered weight also helps keep the hindquarters in relatively the same spot.

The pivot requires no speed on the part of the horse and so requires very gentle cueing from the rider.

When asking the horse to pivot on the forehand instead of the hindquarters, the rider must first fix the bit as a barrier to forward movement. The rider must not pull back on the reins but must shorten them to establish light mouth contact, then push the horse forward to the bit.

When the horse is on the bit properly, the rider will ask for a pivot on the forehand with leg-pressure cues only. If the rider wishes the horse to move his hindquarters to the right around his forehand, he uses left leg pressure back toward the horse's flank. The rider must hold the forehand with the right leg by positioning the right leg forward near the girth. No right leg pressure is required, however. The right leg simply blocks the horse from moving his forehand to the right.

A pivot on the forehand to the left requires the rider to apply opposite leg cues. The horse should be standing relaxed and quiet before the rider requests either forehand or hindquarter pivots. With forward-moving, forehand-hindquarter control exercises, the rider should practice at the jog, which is the easiest gait for the horse. Once these are mastered, the rider can then work the exercises from any gait desired.

8

Cues for More Advanced Riding

ONCE the rider has learned the cues for forehand-hindquarter control exercises and can recognize the feel of the correct response by the horse, he is ready to advance to the sidepass, spin, and flying change of leads.

The sidepass differs from all other western riding exercises in the positioning of the rider's weight. Instead of coming to the rider's weight, the horse must move away from the weight shift if he is to sidepass. This requires special assistance from the rider and a degree of lateral flexibility (spinal arc) by the horse. This bending is also a departure from the usual practice, since the horse's hollow side will be opposite the direction of travel.

In all other riding exercises, the rider shifts his weight into the direction of travel, expecting the horse to move to the weight transfer to bring the team back into balance. But to execute a sidepass, the rider shifts his weight away from the direction of travel in order to apply leg pressure which is slightly firmer than normal. This extra pressure is the added assistance the rider offers in communicating with his partner.

The feel of sidepassing is best learned when the horse is moving slowly. Once the rider has grasped the essential cues and can use those cues with the lightest of touches, he can add speed, but at the beginning the horse should be standing quietly. The rider will lift the reins to inform the horse an action is forthcoming, and when the horse is alert and ready for the next informative cue, the rider will shorten the reins to set the bit as a barrier to forward movement. The rider must use caution and not bump the horse carelessly, shorten the reins too much, which would make the horse shift its weight to its hindquarters, or fail to squeeze the horse gently with both legs to hold the horse's position.

To sidepass to the right, the rider will shift his body weight a bit to the left. This weight transfer must be quite light, so subtle that the horse can feel the change of rider position, but a spectator could not see it.

With the weight shifted, the rider will begin with a minimal lower leg and heel pressure cue to cause the horse's entire body to move away from the pressure. With his weight shifted to the left, the rider will find his right leg has moved completely away from the horse and that there is no contact from the knee down. In this position, there will be virtually no pressure from the rider's right thigh.

As the horse begins to move away from the left leg pressure, the rider may find the horse attempting to turn his head and neck to the right. The rider must hold the head and neck straight and does so with indirect rein pressure. By doing this, he will find that the horse develops minimal lateral flexion away from the direction of travel.

In sidepassing, the horse must cross both the fore and hind legs. If they cross correctly, the left fore and hind legs will move in front of the right legs when the horse is moving to the right. The opposite is the case if the horse is moving to the left. Since it is rather difficult for a horse to cross his legs without striking himself with the crossing leg, the horse will try to lead the sidepass with either the forehand or the hindquarters.

In sidepassing, the horse should be balanced equally on his forehand and hindquarters, so the rider must correct the horse's position with reining cues. If the forehand is starting to

To sidepass correctly, the horse must cross both the fore and hind legs. In moving to the left, the right legs cross over left.

lead, then the rider will use additional direct rein-of-opposition pressure to slow the forehand while the hindquarters are being brought into position. In sidepassing, the rider should move the reining hand sideways in the direction opposite the direction of travel. The rider must avoid any back pull on the rein, as such pressure normally will make the horse shift his weight to the hindquarters.

If the hindquarters start to lead, the rider must speed up the forehand movement rather than retard the speed of the hindquarters. To do this, the rider uses an indirect rein. If the horse is moving to the right and the hindquarters are leading, the rider must bring the forehand into position by indirect rein on the left side of the horse's neck. The horse should seek the center of the reins, moving the forehand more quickly in an attempt to get away from the increased indirect rein pressure.

When sidepassing, the western horse will continue a smooth, steady movement until the rider stops the action. The exercise can be ended by the rider's simply returning his weight to the center of the horse, relaxing the leg pressure, and dropping the reins. The horse should come to rest immediately.

When sidepassing, the rider uses the reining cues to correct any misplacement of the horse's body rather than using leg-pressure cues. Such cues, for the horse, are more closely associated with pivots on the forehand or hindquarters. Since the horse must move his entire body in sidepassing, the rider does not want to run the risk of freezing either the forehand or the hindquarters in place, an action required when requesting a pivot.

The sidepass exercise is also a good one to practice as a preparation for spins, because in sidepassing, the horse comes away from the rider's leg pressure and the indirect rein, actions which are similarly required in spins.

Spins are difficult exercises for many horses, so it is important that the rider select spinning cues which will give the most assistance to the particular horse being worked.

When a horse spins, the sequence of leg movements should be such that there is an equal loading on all four feet, so that the horse is prepared to stop the spin at any point and move off immediately in a straight line.

In spinning to the right, the sequence of leg movement should be a forward step with the right hind foot, then a pushing movement to the right by the horse's left front foot, another sideward pushing movement by the right front foot, and finally, a sideward whipping action by the left hind foot. In the spin, as in the sidepass, the horse's front feet cross.

In order to achieve this action, the rider must set the bit gently to retard forward movement. Then the rider asks the horse to move the right hind foot forward by applying right leg

In a spin to left, the horse's left hind foot begins the action. The right hind foot is last to move and whips horse to the left.

pressure back toward the horse's right flank. In doing so, the rider turns his upper body in the direction of the spin. This twisting movement puts the rider's weight back and to the right, causing the horse's right hind foot to be grounded immediately. The twisting motion also brings the rider's left leg forward where it can apply pressure at the girth. The horse will want to move the forehand away from this pressure.

To squeeze harder with the legs, the rider should attempt to push his inside hip forward. (In a spin to the right, it would be the right hip.) This action tightens the rider's thigh muscles. The rider must also use a fairly strong and consistent indirect rein cue to tell the horse to seek the center of the reins. The horse will tilt his head and neck in the direction of travel, pur-

The rider twists upper body to the left, hips to the right to establish spin cues and bring legs into natural spin position.

suing the center of the reins until the exercise is ended, when the rider relieves the indirect rein pressure. The rider should not let the horse "rubberneck" — swing the head and neck too far to avoid moving the forehand. The rider must also be careful not to pull back on the reins, as this makes the horse overload his hindquarters and possibly back out of the spin.

With some horses, the rider may find it is necessary to use a slightly different set of cues to spin correctly. Because of conformation or weakness in the hindquarters, many horses have a tendency to swing their hindquarters out, away from the direction of the spin.

If this is the case, then the rider must hold the hindquarters in place. For example, in a spin to the right, the horse may

If the horse has a tendency to swing hindquarters into the spin, rider may reverse leg cues, using outside leg to hold hindquarters.

swing his hindquarters to the left. Ordinarily, the rider's left leg would be positioned forward to push the forehand to the right, but if it is necessary to assist the horse further to hold the hindquarters, the rider moves the left leg back toward the flank and applies strong pressure. In doing so, the rider will find that his right leg comes away from the horse. This is to be expected and is acceptable as long as the rider is careful not to let his right leg accidentally bump the horse's forehand, which is moving to the right in response to the indirect left rein pressure.

As with all other western riding exercises, once the rider has initiated the exercise and is sure the horse understands what is expected of him, then the rider must relinquish control to the horse. If the horse is given freedom to complete the exercise, he'll do so in good form. It is when the rider attempts to force speed or fails to yield control that the horse backs out of the spin, swaps ends, jumps around, or throws his head up.

The leg and body weight-shift cues inform the horse of what is expected, and they define the direction. These cues should be continued lightly throughout the exercise as they help the rider remain in balance with the horse rather than falling behind the movement. The responsive western horse will continue the spin until he is allowed to reach the center of the reins, at which time he'll expect the rider to stop leg and weight cues.

With some horses, the rider may find it easier to get the correct form in a spin if he starts the exercise with sidepassing cues. If the rider wishes to spin to the right, he can first cue the horse to sidepass to the right. As the horse begins the sidepass movement to the right, the rider should change to the spin cues and apply strong indirect left rein pressure. The momentum started by sidepassing to the right will carry the horse into the spin and the horse will have an easier time getting started.

The flying change of leads is a natural movement for the horse. In this exercise the rider must be extremely careful to apply cues judiciously. Too strong a cue will cause the horse to overreact in an attempt to please the rider.

A brief summary of the movement of the horse's legs at the lope will show us why the timing of cues is so important in getting the horse to change leads smoothly while advancing.

The lope on the left lead is a three-beat gait in which the action is initiated by the horse's right hind foot. The second beat of the gait is the left hind foot and the right forefoot moving together, and the third beat is the leading left forefoot.

Just as the leading left forefoot is being grounded, the horse has both hind feet off the ground for a brief moment. This is the moment when the rider must cue for the flying change of leads.

To put the horse on the left lead, the rider must ask the horse

Lead changes are natural and correct if rider makes request as the leading leg is grounded and both hind feet are in air.

to move the right hind foot forward, with right leg pressure applied just slightly back toward the horse's flank.

The rider shifts his weight back and to the right, in order to establish a shortened right stride, and allows his left leg to move slightly forward toward the horse's left shoulder. This is a natural movement by the rider and precedes the natural extension of the horse's muscles on the left side.

The rider should allow very gentle indirect right rein pressure to inform the horse the direction of travel will be to the left.

When the horse is on the left lead, all of the horse's muscles on the left side are extended. This twists the rider's body and pushes his left shoulder somewhat forward.

In this position, the rider should be able to feel that the horse

The first beat of the lope on left lead is the placement of the right hind foot. The right hind foot moves forward on a short stride. The second beat is the left hind and right forefoot moving together. The third beat is the left forefoot being placed on the long stride. The change must be made now, while both hindfeet are off the ground. In the middle right photo, the left hind is being grounded first, so the new sequence of movement will produce a right lead. In the final photo the horse is on the right lead and completing the three-beat sequence with a long right foreleg stride.

is on the correct lead. It should never be necessary for the rider to look down at the horse's shoulder or to lean forward to look for the leading foreleg. To do either puts both horse and rider out of the correct and natural position for the exercise.

Timing is the most critical element in requesting a flying change of leads. If the rider asks too soon or too late, the horse is not in a position to make the change in a single sequence of leg movements. If the rider's timing is off, the horse will often change in front, but fail to make the change behind until the following lope sequence.

The rider must ask for the change just before the leading foreleg is grounded, so the horse has the opportunity to make the change behind first, then complete the lope sequence with a change of leads in front.

So, as the leading foreleg moves forward, the rider gently shifts his weight from one side to the other. If the horse is then on the left lead, the weight shift will be from the right side to the left side. As the transfer is being made, the rider must let his legs follow naturally, the left leg going back and the right leg moving forward. The rider now removes indirect right rein pressure gently and applies indirect left rein pressure to inform the horse of the change in direction.

All of the cues are given simultaneously. The rein cue, however, should be delayed just long enough to make sure it is the last cue given.

The shift in the rider's weight causes the horse's left hind foot to be grounded first. The rider's left leg pressure informs the horse that the left hind leg is to pick up the driving action required for continuing the gait, and the indirect left rein pressure tells the horse a new direction of travel is desired. If properly done, the change of leads will take place in a single sequence of the three beats, the horse changing both front and rear feet in the same sequence.

For some reason, riders often attempt to force the flying change. Such force almost always ends with the horse resenting the exercise, and the horse expresses his resentment by speeding up, wringing his tail, throwing his head up, or combining all these faults.

All that is required is that the rider inform the horse with gentle cues, then give the horse the freedom necessary to respond. No forced, harshly demanded flying change will be as smooth and graceful as the horse's natural change.

9

Negotiating Trail Course Obstacles

THE POSITION of the rider's body is crucial in all phases of western riding, but never more important than when negotiating tight trail course obstacles.

The trail horse is a special kind of western horse. He must have a calm disposition and the correct mental attitude about his work. He must be eager to learn new things, must be fresh and alert, and above all, he must be trained to respond immediately to the faintest cue.

The rider can help a potential trail horse be all these things if the rider's mental attitude is also correct. However, he must understand that the good western trail horse was probably born with most of his talent. The knowledgeable rider can cultivate that talent, shape and polish it, and help the horse shine. By giving his mount confidence, the good western rider can help any horse through the obstacles and can help any horse perform, but he must realize he can never make a champion trail horse out of a horse that doesn't have the "want to."

The lack of "want to" seems to be most easily observed in the trail horse. The nature of the work the trail horse is asked to do in the show ring places limitations on how much the rider can help the horse. Even a good rider can't use the impulsion generated by speed to get through a turn, for all obstacles in trail classes are worked with gentleness and lightness. The rider can't use bit leverage to bring the horse to a stop, nor can he coerce the horse across a stream. If the horse doesn't want to, there's not too much the rider can do.

It is not until the rider has mastered all the control cues and learned to take a natural, relaxed seat that trail obstacles can be tackled. The rider who uses a stiff equitation position will find it impossible to help the horse through the obstacles. Only a relaxed rider, willing to bend, move, turn, stand, and lean, can position the horse correctly, can communicate his desires, and can relinquish control to a confident, calm, relaxed horse.

Because the key to natural western riding is the communication and freedom which exists between the partners, this becomes particularly important when the horse and rider are working with trail class obstacles.

There is also a secret to getting a superior performance from the trail horse. It is to let the horse study the obstacle and make the final decision. The rider reveals his understanding of the secret by giving the horse all the time he needs and by not forcing the horse into wrong positions that make it difficult for him to complete the exercises.

A well-schooled western trail horse knows what is to be done, and he'll accomplish it if he's given the time to figure out just how he wants to do it. The western trail horse has been taught to move only on command, to stop on command, and to arc, back, sidepass, pivot, and jump. He'll respond to all of the rider's requests, even if those requests are incorrect for a particular situation. But if the partnership is a good one, the rider will not try to make all the decisions. Instead, he'll give the horse time to review the obstacle first, then will initiate the body positioning necessary for the horse to work the obstacle, and finally, will let the horse complete the work in his own good time.

The obstacles chosen for the trail course are designed to prove the horse's calmness, his ability to work, and the rider's mastery of control. Most commonly, the obstacles include, but are not limited to, gates, bridges, water, tarps, tires, logs, barrels, domestic animals, and a variety of weights which the horse must pull. The rider's control of the horse is demonstrated by forward movement, slow spins on the forehand and hindquarters, backing, and sidepassing. The horse's ability is demonstrated in the way he responds to the rider's requests and the manner in which he handles himself before, during, and after an obstacle has been worked.

A common trail course obstacle is the low jump, which may be worked either with the rider mounted or on the ground.

If the rider is required to dismount and lead the horse over the jump obstacle, the rider should dismount naturally rather than using the equitation dismount. Once off the horse, the rider will slip the closed reins over the horse's head and gather the romal by folding it in the right hand. If split reins are being used, the rider should hold both reins in his right hand. The rider remains on the left side of the horse and should never get in front of the horse.

When leading the horse over a jump, the rider will normally take the jump first, looking back immediately to see the positioning of the horse. It is quite important that the rider does not pull or jerk on the reins, which would bang the bit around in the horse's mouth. One harsh jerk and the horse will stop before taking the jump.

Normally, the rider walks or jogs to the obstacle and then steps over it, so the horse does not have a greal deal of impulsion. The rider must keep walking once he has made the jump, indicating to the horse it is necessary for the horse to clear the obstacle before stopping. All too often the rider gets over the jump, then stops and waits for the horse. When the rider stops, the horse, as taught, also stops.

But if the horse has jumped the obstacle successfully, the rider stops the horse within a few feet. The rider then remounts, again using the natural style rather than the artificial equitation style.

In taking a jump obstacle with the western horse, the rider must never pull the horse, but should direct the horse gently.

If the jump is to be taken with the rider mounted, the rider's primary responsibility is to provide guidance and confidence by consistent light leg pressure and neck and head freedom by slack reins.

In classic riding, it would be a mistake for the rider of a jumper to drop the reins just before a jump, abandoning the horse to work on his own just at the time he needs the most assistance. But the western horse, which is not jumping for height, always prefers the freedom to finish the exercise on his own, so dropping the reins just before the horse tackles a low obstacle is the correct move. Also, dropping or lengthening the reins on the western horse protects the horse's mouth from accidently being bruised by the bit.

The western rider should keep in mind that he is not on a fox hunt or in a jumping class, so the horse does not need the impulsion gained by strong, driving cues from the rider's legs.

Instead, the western rider, upon approaching the jump, should stand lightly in the stirrups, and squeeze with both legs to tell the horse he wants both forward movement and a jump to clear the obstacle. The rider should lengthen the reins to give the necessary freedom and rely on the horse's desire to remain in the center of the reins as a means of controlling direction.

Immediately after taking the jump, the rider should sit down in the saddle, resuming the natural seat of a western rider at rest. Such action should be a sufficient cue to stop the trail horse. When the rider is ready to work the next obstacle test, the rider will lift the reins, telling the horse action is about to begin again.

Another trail course obstacle, gates, requires the horse to sidepass and back. The rule of gates for the rider is: If the gate

In working gates, the western horse should properly position the rider by working close to the gate and parallel to it.

swings away from the team, the horse should be moved through the gate in a forward motion. If the gate swings toward the team, the horse should be backed through the gate. If the gate swings both ways and the rider has been given no instruction as to how it is to be worked, he may make a decision based on his knowledge of how the horse works best.

Normally, the rider walks the horse at right angles to the gate. Upon reaching the gate, the horse should be stopped and turned parallel to the fence line by either pivoting on the hindquarters or pivoting on the forehand. The most important thing to remember in bringing the horse parallel to the gate is to position the horse's feet correctly. The horse should never stand at an angle to the gate, forcing the rider to lean out of position in order to unlatch the gate. The horse should be moved carefully into position, crossing his front or hind feet properly as he swings either the forehand or the hindquarters into place.

Once the horse is in the proper position, the rider should relax all cues, letting the horse rest for a moment. Then the rider picks up the reins, shortening them yet leaving enough length for the horse to move forward. If the rider wants to hold the horse, he can twist his wrist and set the bit as a barrier. If the rider is using closed reins, he will gather the romal in the left hand, freeing his right hand to work the gate, or vice versa, depending on direction.

Once the rider has grasped the gate, he cannot let go. Therefore, it is imperative he keep the horse in an advantageous position at all times. The horse will cooperate if given ample time to position himself and if the rider uses gentle, consistent leg cues.

A common mistake is that the rider abandons the leg cues in favor of leaning over in the saddle to reach the gate. Once the rider starts to lean, the horse reacts by coming to the rider's weight too quickly, or the horse may think a sidepass was indicated, and he will move away from the weight shift. The

The western rider never abandons cues or leans out to compensate for the horse's poor position. The horse is moved to the gate.

rider will avoid what seems like a necessity to lean and stretch his arm if he'll let the top rail of the gate slide through his fingers as his horse moves either forward or back.

As the horse is ridden forward through the gate, the rider pushes the gate away and keeps the horse moving forward until the rider's knee which is closest to the gate has passed the end of the gate. At this point, the rider stops the horse. The rider turns the horse's forehand to the right, around the end of the gate, by using indirect rein pressure on the left side of the horse's neck. At the same time, the rider moves the horse's hindquarters to the left by applying right leg pressure back on the horse's flank. Once the horse has been turned around and again is in a position parallel to the fence line (but facing in the opposite direction), the rider asks the horse to sidepass, making it possible for the rider to close the gate.

If the horse must be backed through the gate, the rider should move the horse into a parallel position to the fence line with the horse facing the hinged end of the gate. The rider's knee should be just opposite the gate latch. The rider opens the latch and must sidepass the horse away from the fence line. When the gate has been opened just wide enough to give the horse room to move through, the horse is pivoted on the forehand, bringing the hindquarters into the gate opening. As the horse backs through the gate, the hindquarters should be pushed gently into a parallel line with the fence.

As the horse backs through the gate opening, it will be necessary for the rider to let the top rail of the gate slip through his hand to compensate for the new positioning of the horse. Once the gate has been closed, the rider moves the horse forward to latch and secure the gate.

The gate obstacle is said to be well executed if the horse and rider take their time, the horse positions himself so the rider does not have to lean from the saddle, and the gate is opened no more than necessary to let the horse and rider pass through.

When approaching a trail course obstacle which is below the horse's knees, the rider should give the horse an opportunity to inspect the situation thoroughly before being asked to move.

Whether being walked, jogged, or loped to an obstacle, the horse must be stopped before the obstacle is worked. Once he has stopped the horse, the rider relaxes the reins, telling the horse the team is at rest. A horse at rest is not being asked to inspect an obstacle, and the rider should not expect the horse to study the upcoming test. Therefore, the rider must pick up the reins to alert the horse to the fact that work is about to begin. Then the rider can gently "toss out" some rein, giving the horse both the cue and the freedom to put his head down and study the obstacle.

The horse will inform the rider that he is through examining the obstacle by lifting his head, or by looking off in another direction, seemingly no longer interested in the job ahead. It is then time for the rider to shorten the reins to request either the walk, jog, or lope.

Negotiating bridges in the trail class requires the rider to shorten the rein, informing the horse the rider wishes the horse to walk. Then the rider squeezes with both legs, driving the horse forward, and simultaneously lengthens the rein so that the horse can see the structure on which he is about to step. The sound of his hoofs striking a wooden or metal bridge may disturb the horse, so the rider should not shorten the reins or make any movement which might confuse the horse and make him think some new action is being requested. The rider should remain quiet and again give the horse the cue to walk forward. If the rider holds this cue, usually the horse will regain his confidence and proceed to answer the rider's request.

Water obstacles often pose problems for trail class riders. After the horse has had an opportunity to study the obstacle, the rider must give the horse all the usual cues to proceed at a particular gait. When water obstacles are involved, or when tarps, pieces of plastic, paper, or other objects which rattle, blow, or move when the horse steps upon them are used, it is the rider's responsibility to give the horse confidence. He does this by maintaining a relaxed, natural position, giving the horse additional freedom from the reins, and applying light, but constant, leg pressure.

Walking a horse through a series of tires, or over poles which have been placed at angles so that the horse must step in and out, means the rider must give the horse sufficient rein so the horse can get his head down and turn it for a better view of the obstacle.

There is no time limit for most trail classes, so it is almost always the rider's errors which cause the horse to make mistakes with obstacles which require careful placement of the horse's feet. The horse can, and will, put his feet in the tires or

When working obstacles below the horse's knee, the rider must free the horse so the horse can look at the obstacle, then proceed.

between the poles if the rider gives him time and freedom to see what he is doing. The horse does best with his head down, a position which calls for complete freedom from bit pressure.

Working around domesticated animals as part of the trail course requires the rider to keep the horse's attention on the direction and style of travel. In this case, the rider must not give the horse complete freedom to look around, but must keep the horse alert to rider cues. The rider should play with the reins gently, keeping the horse interested in what is about to happen rather than in whatever animal is nearby, whether it is a pig or goat.

Backing through an L-shaped course or around barrels is quite easy for the horse if the rider remembers to give gentle,

The trail course rider must lean forward or backward or to one side to determine positioning of the horse, then ask for movement.

In backing around or through obstacles, errors are most often made by the rider who rushes the horse. Look, then ask horse to move.

understandable cues and does not get his upper body out of position, which the horse could interpret as a weight shift and respond accordingly. However, when working any obstacle which requires the horse to back a single, careful step at a time, the rider must shift his weight back and to the side in order to freeze a hind foot in place.

The rider should not lean forward trying to see how the horse is doing with the obstacle. Instead, the rider should shift the weight back, then look down. The rider's weight on the horse's hindquarters keeps the hind feet grounded and prevents the animal from bumping the obstacle needlessly. The rider should also be careful that in looking back he doesn't move the reins unconsciously, giving the indirect rein cue which could make the horse move sideways.

Almost all errors made by the horse on obstacles which require the horse to back are really rider errors. And in almost every case, it has to do with the fact that the rider failed to give the horse all the time he needed. A rider simply cannot rush a horse in this class.

Rider error also accounts for the most common problems horses have in sidepassing over an obstacle. The rider cues the horse correctly for the sidepass but fails to position the horse properly in relation to the obstacle to be negotiated. The rider fails to remember that the center of the horse is just behind the rider, not under him, so when sidepassing up to an obstacle, the rider mistakenly lines up the obstacle under himself, when it should be just behind his back.

Now, the horse can still sidepass over an obstacle which is directly opposite the rider, but the chances for error are much greater. If the obstacle is positioned just behind the rider, the obstacle is actually an equal distance from the horse's front and hind feet.

Pulling obstacles such as logs or tires is no problem to the trained western horse if the rider will remain relaxed and give consistent, mild cues. The horse needs to know he is doing well when he is pulling something and his confidence in himself depends on a strong rider who knows how to be gentle.

The rider of a trail horse may choose to wear spurs, since spurs make it easier for the rider to reach the proper cue position on the horse's sides, eliminating the need for any shift of weight which might misinform the horse. Spurs also assure greater accuracy in cue placement. For example, if the rider wants to move only the horse's hindquarters, the spur gives more reach to the rider's leg so the cue can be placed well back toward the flank.

The natural western seat is never more appreciated than when the rider works the horse on trail class obstacles, for when relaxed yet alert and responsive work is required of both members of the team, the flexibility of the natural western seat makes the job much easier for horse and rider.

10

Reining the Western Horse

THE TRUE western horse is a "reining" horse, and because he is, he must "pack a bridle." The term "reining" does not mean that the horse competes in a reining class or that he is necessarily a stock horse. It means that the western horse responds first to rein cues; second, to bit cues. And "packing a bridle" does not mean the horse is "on the bit" or "collected" or "has his head tucked."

The western horse which packs a bridle receives part of his information through the bit, is sensitive and responsive to the bit, holds the bit, and yet carries himself in a natural, balanced manner.

Such definitions are sure to cause controversy, and therefore need further elaboration.

The cue sequence for exercises has been given in this order: verbal command, the weight shift, leg pressure, and finally, the reining cue. However, it has been stated clearly that before the rider initiates any action, the reins must be picked up, alerting the horse to the fact that further communication will be forthcoming.

Prior to any action leading to any exercise, the rider communicates with the horse through the reins. The rider may or may not then use a verbal command to indicate the chosen gait, follow that cue with pressure from the leg to reinforce the verbal command or with a shift of weight to determine foot position and/or direction, and possibly apply additional pressure with the leg to continue the driving action of the horse's hindquarters or to move the forehand.

The key cue, however, is always one involving the reins. This cue not only completes the rider's obligation of providing full instruction concerning the work expected, but also initiates the horse's assumption of control so he can finish the requested action naturally.

It is the reining cue which relinquishes control to the horse and the horse's subsequent action of seeking the center of the reins which make the western horse a "reining" horse. In contrast, the classically trained horse is never free of the rider's control, much of which is directed through the reins.

Rein cues are always the first and last communication between rider and horse. The rein cue precedes all other cues in alerting the horse to work. It is the cue which transfers control from rider to horse. It is the final cue which ends all work and puts the horse at rest.

To "pack a bridle," the horse must hold the bit in his mouth. In so doing, he becomes sensitive to the mouthpiece of the bit. His response to the bit is a learned response, never a forced response. He carries himself in a balanced, natural way because he is ready and willing to work and to please a partner, a state he will never reach if he is under severe restraint or excessive pressures.

The western horse can "pack a bridle" and be "on the bit" at the same time. But he can also hold the bit, be sensitive and respond to it, and yet not be "on the bit." The distinction is in the change of control. The western horse should be on the bit while the rider is in control. He'll be off the bit when he is in control, for when the horse controls the action, the horse is free.

The western horse can be collected and, in many cases, will be. But when he is, he'll most often be under the control of the

The horse is collected when his natural balance point has been moved from in front of, to under the rider. The horse must move to the bit.

When the horse is collected he will be on the bit and will remain so on his own as long as rider doesn't change weight position.

rider rather than working on his own. Collection requires the movement of the horse's balance point from its natural position behind and above the horse's elbow to under the rider. This is accomplished by setting the bit to establish a barrier, then driving the horse's hindquarters forward. This results in the horse's relaxing his back, shortening his neck and shoulder muscles, relaxing the jaw, and flexing at the poll. When he has repositioned himself in response to the rider's request, the horse will have shifted his balance point under the rider and will be in a state of collection.

The horse can, and does, assume a collected state on his own. After the horse has taken control and is working on his own, he has two things to think about — finishing the exercise requested and carrying the rider's weight. The good western horse will try to keep the rider's weight balanced. To do so, he must move to the rider's weight and he must keep his balance point under the rider if he is to continue the exercise with any degree of smoothness. He therefore collects himself.

It is for this reason the rider must lead the horse with a weight shift. The rider must "get there" first. If the rider should fall behind the horse, the horse will often hesitate or even stop an exercise. The horse cannot collect himself as he moves through the exercise if he must go back to reposition a rider.

The finished western horse works on a curb bit, and selection of the bit is of prime importance to the rider, for while the western horse will usually work on any type of bit, the correct one clarifies communication.

The curb bit can have any number of different mouthpieces.

The horse can remain collected only if the rider leads him into turns or the next exercise, then allows the horse freedom.

It is called a curb because it has a curb strap, or chain, which applies pressure to the chin groove of the horse when the reins are shortened.

The curb bit has a cheekpiece above the mouthpiece and a shank below the mouthpiece. The headstall and the curb strap attach to the upper cheekpiece, while the reins attach at the lower end of the shank. The curb bit is said to be solid-jawed if the shank and cheekpiece have no lateral movement. When the shank and cheekpiece are movable, the bit is called loose-jawed.

There are some strong opinions about the choice of the loose- or solid-jawed bit. Those favoring the loose-jawed bit generally claim greater allowance for rider mistakes. Since the cheeks of the bit move, the hand of an unsteady rider does not accidentally communicate unwanted signals. The design also reduces the severity of the bit.

Proponents of the solid-jawed bit claim the bit is a better communicative tool since the slightest movement of the bit is a direct signal to the horse.

Both arguments have merit. However, I believe correcting mistakes made with either bit is not done by changing the bit, but by improving the rider.

The lengths of the cheekpiece and shank of the bit, in concert with the mouthpiece, determine the severity of the bit. A short-shanked bit with a low cheekpiece will generally be a milder bit than a long-shanked bit. The longer the shank, the greater the leverage which can be applied by a pull on the reins. A medium-shanked bit with a high cheekpiece can be terribly severe, since the high cheekpiece movement exerts greater pressure on the poll through the headstall and on the chin groove through the chin strap. The rider should examine both the length of the shank and the length of the cheekpiece before making a determination about the amount of rein pressure which can be applied.

Usually when riders talk about the mildness or severity of

bits, they are thinking of the mouthpiece of the bit. A bit which is easy on the horse's mouth is one which has a straight bar. The bar mouthpiece rests primarily on the horse's tongue, keeping the bars of the mouth from taking the full weight of the bit.

Another mild bit is the mullen mouthpiece, which has a curved bar (back to front and sometimes bottom to top). The low port mouthpiece is also a gentle bit, although the port relieves some of the bit weight from the tongue, transferring it to the bars of the mouth.

The finished western horse works most frequently on a half-breed or similar bit. The half-breed is a straight bar mouthpiece with a cricket and roller. If it is balanced properly, this bit lies comfortably in the horse's mouth, has sufficient weight to help bring the horse's head into a vertical position, and is large enough to communicate a cue quickly even when the reins are moved only a little.

The spade bit is most commonly associated with the western horse. Unfortunately, it has wrongly been the target of much criticism — in the right hands it can be an instrument for the highest form of subtle communication. The spade has a cricket with roller, a large spoon or spade at the top of the cricket, and concave wires above the straight bar mouthpiece to lower the bit in the horse's mouth. If it is improperly jerked about, it can do quite a bit of damage to the horse's mouth. However, the bit is not the source of the problem. The problem is with the rider attached to the other end of the reins.

The slightest change in the bit position is felt by the horse and the horse responds. Clearly, only the best-trained western horse should ever carry a spade bit, and only the most knowledgeable rider should ever attempt to use one. It should never be used as a pain inflicter to punish a misbehaving horse. It should never be used just so the rider can overpower the horse. But used properly on the finished horse, the spade will relay a message from rider to horse in the quickest and gentlest way.

You may hear some novice western riders speak of putting a

bit in a horse's mouth only on occasion and, when doing so, using only the gentlest of bits. They believe this will "save" the horse's mouth, keeping it soft and responsive to stimulation. What they say may be true, but it is wrong. The good western horse has an educated mouth because he carries the bit so frequently that it is second nature to him, and contrary to what the novice rider thinks, a bit which fits properly and is used correctly "makes" the horse's mouth.

Yes, keeping a bit out of the horse's mouth "saves" it, but only from an education.

Three points to keep in mind when selecting a bit are: Rollers in a bit soften the bit's action when the reins are shortened. Copper rollers or a copper mouthpiece make the horse salivate, which keeps the mouth moist and more sensitive to the bit. Generally, horses like iron bits better than ones of stainless steel or aluminum.

The mouthpiece of a western bit is generally 4½ to 5½ inches in width. The bit is too narrow when the cheeks or lips of the horse are pinched or rubbed by the bit shanks or cheekpieces. The bit is too wide if the cheeks and shanks do not rest close to the horse's skin.

The diameter of the mouthpiece determines whether the bit is mild or severe. If the mouthpiece is thin, the bit is severe. If the diameter of the mouthpiece is larger, the weight of the bit is spread over a greater area in the horse's mouth, and therefore the bit is milder.

The bit is positioned properly in the horse's mouth when it rests at any point on the bars of the mouth. In fact, I like to use as much of the bars of the mouth as possible and therefore frequently raise and lower the bit in the mouth. However, a bit is often too high in the mouth when there are wrinkles at the corner of the horse's lips, and it is too low if the mouthpiece hits or rests too close to the tushes.

The curb strap is part of the communication system of the bit and it should not be too loose. The curb strap should make contact with the horse by the time the shank has been moved back 30 degrees. To avoid any strap contact is to condone greater movement of the bit, which, in turn, encourages riders to pull back harder on the reins or to shorten the reins to a greater extent.

The weight of the bit and the way it is balanced in the horse's mouth help determine the horse's head position. The horse with an "educated" mouth responds to the weight of the bit and brings his head to a near vertical position to eliminate the weight. When the horse lowers his head to this position, the weight of the bit is suspended from the headstall and is no longer carried on the bars of the mouth. When the horse is pushed to the bit, the bars of the mouth remain in contact with the mouthpiece.

A bit that is light in weight permits the horse to hold his nose out, since there is little weight being felt on the tongue and bars of the mouth, while he must drop his nose to free his mouth from the weight of a heavy bit.

Over-bitting a horse is more common than under-bitting, since weighting the horse with a heavy bit is the path of least resistance when the rider is really incompetent. Rather than learn the techniques of proper western riding, which include balance and poise and gentleness toward the animal, the rider grabs for a larger bit, hoping to get better control. What the rider gets is a horse which is uncomfortable and eventually shows his displeasure with all work because any kind of work becomes punishment.

The rider who over-bits his horse lacks self-confidence and therefore cannot work with a partner, giving the horse full control when the partner has the greater talent. And the rider who abuses his horse physically and verbally is the poorest rider of all. That rider is fearful, and while his display of force and aggressive action may relieve some of his anxiety, it is completely wrong in the eyes of the skilled horseman.

Whether the rider uses Texas or California style of reining, he should hold the reins lightly between the thumb and index

The advanced western horse needs weight and leg cues to initiate action, but finishes on the rein cue as he seeks the center of the reins.

To shorten the reins, California style, the rider lifts the right hand, then gently and smoothly pulls the reins through the left hand.

finger of the reining hand. The remaining fingers of the reining hand are spread naturally in a relaxed position and they are used to play gently upon the reins.

If the rider uses Texas-style reining, he may not touch the reins with the off hand, and therefore must inch his reining hand down the reins. In my opinion, this rule is both silly and unsafe, but until it is changed, the rider must struggle with the reins if he is in the show ring. If he is using this style of reining outside the show ring, the rider can, and should, use the off hand to pull the reins through the reining hand. This is exactly what is done when a rider uses the California style of reining, in which the romal is held in the off hand.

If, when using the California style of reining, the rider should wish to use a gentle bumping action to remind the horse to keep his head positioned, then he need only bump the reins with his free fingers. If the rider moves these fingers quickly toward his stomach and then relaxes them immediately, the sensitive horse will get the message. It isn't necessary for the rider to twist his wrist or pull on the reins to bump the horse.

As I have previously pointed out, the major difference between riding in the classic manner and riding western is the freedom given the western horse. Mouth contact is essential when riding a classically trained horse. The elimination of mouth contact is essential when riding the western-trained horse.

Lack of mouth contact does not mean the horse is to be permitted to move out of position or beyond the rider's control. It simply means the horse is to be given freedom once he has demonstrated that he understands the rider's request and is willing to assume control over the completion of the exercise.

The western rider will tell the horse what is expected by presenting the proper cues and then let the reins go slack so that when the horse is in the proper position to complete the exercise, he is carrying the bit in a natural position. When the horse is correctly positioned and is performing the requested exercise and is holding the bit properly, there is no bit pressure being applied by the rider. By its own design and weight, the bit is helping the horse to hold a balanced position, yet the horse is free of control by the rider.

The good western rider will not use the bit and reins to force the horse into a position which is unnatural for his bodily structure. Because of conformation, some horses can flex easily at the poll and be very comfortable carrying their heads in the vertical position. Others, however, are simply not physically capable of working in that position. The short, heavy-necked horse can carry his head and neck low, but he'll have difficulty carrying his head in a vertical position. He should not be forced to do so, but should be allowed to work at his most comfortable position.

Natural western riding demands some intelligence and knowledge on the part of the rider. The rider does not attempt to adhere blindly to artificial standards, either for himself or the horse. Instead, the good rider studies the conformation of his horse, then assists the horse as much as he can to assume the best and most natural working position for that particular horse.

Good western riding on a reining horse which "packs a bridle" requires the rider to participate as a full partner in the accomplishment of an exercise. It also requires the rider to free the horse at the proper time, giving him the best opportunity to work naturally, smoothly, and willingly in response to the rider's requests.

If the rider allows the reins to remain relaxed, the advanced horse will carry himself properly, and the bit will be correctly positioned.

11

Riding in the Show Ring

IT IS THE OBVIOUS which frequently goes unnoticed, and so it is with the horse's physical structure. Many riders look at the horse's conformation in terms of current standards of beauty, but few riders view the horse with thoughts of function. Unfortunately, it seems that at today's western horse shows, too great an emphasis is placed on the good-looking, flashy horse rather than on the horse that moves or functions well. That striking stallion with the golden coat and the four white socks may not move through the prescribed routine nearly as well as the quiet little bay horse, yet he may be declared the class winner.

Such inequities are probably the reason real horsemen abide by the old adage "Pretty is as pretty does."

The skeletal structure and muscle system of the horse provide most adequately for special athletic abilities. At the same time, these physical attributes limit the horse for other kinds of movement. For example, the horse has virtually no lateral movement of the legs. His body is designed for speed in straight flight. This fact is an asset in the performance of some exercises, yet it is a disadvantage when lateral movements, such as spins or sidepasses, are required.

The natural western rider tries to understand both the limitations and the capabilities of the horse, and the natural rider therefore uses verbal commands, weight shifts, leg aids, and rein cues in concert with the horse's physical structure. The natural western rider avoids putting his horse in a poor position because it is his responsibility to make it as easy as possible for the horse to complete the requested exercise. The natural western rider never attempts to force activity which is prohibited by the horse's anatomy. Instead, he frees the horse so the horse can complete the work in his best natural position.

The limitations imposed by the horse's body make a single movement correct and all other movements incorrect in the accomplishment of a particular exercise. Because there is only one correct way for the horse to perform each exercise, the correct performance is one which exerts the least stress on the horse's body and his mental capacity.

Horses become champions at particular events because they are naturally superior at that type of work. This is the reason breeders attempt to improve the horse's conformation and disposition for specialized work. Some horses are naturally better than others. Some have a greater ability to work cattle. Some spin better, some stop better, and some work trail obstacles better than others. The trainer teaches the horse to respond to cues and to position himself for the individual exercises, and the rider makes every effort to assist the horse in reaching his potential, but when all is said and done, the horse must demonstrate a natural superiority at the task if he is to be victorious in competition.

The western rider who uses the natural-seat method understands this and consequently knows that the correct position for the rider is the position which interferes least with the horse's effort to perform as asked. This then becomes the goal of the natural western rider.

On the other hand, the western rider who uses the formal, rigid equitation style is guided by a set of artificial standards and often disregards entirely the stress he places on his horse as he tries to keep the rigid, upright, centered position. This position is an attempt to copy the seat used by riders of a classically trained horse. It is the incorrect way to ride and work the western horse, which is not under the rider's control at all times.

The western horse is asked to work free of rider control and often with a great deal of speed. The classically trained horse is always under the rider's control and works with a deliberate cadence. He is never asked for his natural speed or given complete freedom. The rider of the classically trained horse can remain in the center of his horse's movement because the horse is under his control and responds only to his requests. The conditioned responses are rated, slow, and precise.

This rider's horse is "on the bit," and the rider most often uses a full bridle, two hands on four reins, and a crop or whip as an accessory aid. It is very different for the western rider. He lets the horse work off the bit, uses one hand on the reins, and does not use a whip as an aid.

The conformation sought in the classic horse is different from that sought in a western horse.

The performance desired from each is different.

The riding styles should therefore be different.

But some people too readily seek the approval of their peers, and like lemmings, many riders plunge into the show ring with a good western horse and a foreign riding style.

With this in mind, the natural western rider enters the show ring seated on his horse in a relaxed, poised manner. However, the posture, even though natural, will be different for each rider, for we know that each rider, like each horse, is an individual.

What is being sought in western competition is a display of the horse's natural ability to perform. The good rider, seeking to show off his horse and accepting the fact that he does not have the same physical characteristics as his competitor, should avoid any attempt to copy the way the competition is seated and should concentrate instead on helping his horse.

Indeed, rider ego must be subordinated, if only for a few moments, to allow a place for pride in the horse's effort. In fact, if the rider would only make it a practice to transfer his primary concern from himself to his horse, he would virtually assume the best natural western riding position without too much thought.

When riding the natural western seat in the western pleasure class, for example, the rider will sit tall in the saddle on the front part of his inner thighs, with his legs slightly forward, his knees and lower legs close to the horse, and his heels down. This is the position which is most natural for a completely relaxed rider who is desirous of assisting his horse.

A tall, slender rider with long legs will find leg cues relatively easy to give to assist the horse. The long-legged rider does not have to think much about keeping his legs close to the horse's sides. His build naturally places his legs in the correct position, as long as he remains relaxed. This rider will soon find his legs are his most natural aid, and he will use them as his primary cue.

The rider whose legs are shorter will find giving leg cues more difficult. This rider can compensate for his size by wearing spurs, which make the placement of cues easier. The shorter rider should ride a horse well suited to his size, avoiding any horse which is too heavy-bodied. This rider will find that his chief asset is his upper body weight, and this becomes his most useful aid in cueing rather than his legs.

The natural western rider will avoid tensing his body with the same degree of concern he uses in avoiding putting any unnecessary stress on the horse's body.

When riding around the ring, the rider will look forward, not just to keep his chin up, but for the more important purpose of knowing what lies ahead. The rider's off hand will be carried naturally at his side, rather than waving aimlessly about and disrupting the horse. And the rider's reining hand will hold the reins lightly at a level which gives the horse freedom yet is accessible for quick communication. The rider should never let his reining hand get too high, for this tends to lift the horse's forehand, causing him to move out of position.

If the rider sits as described, the bit will hang naturally in the horse's mouth, and the horse will carry his neck and head in the most natural position dictated by his conformation and style of moving.

At West Coast shows, the horse is expected to "pack the bridle" by holding his head in a near vertical position. In the Midwest, North, South, and on the East Coast, the horse is generally allowed greater freedom of head and neck carriage, and in these areas, horses are not trained and shown with their heads tucked to the vertical. They usually carry their necks so the top line is parallel to the ground. The West Coast horse, on the other hand, is required to arch his neck to some degree to achieve the "tucked" look.

Either style is correct as long as the rider lets the horse position himself according to his conformation, thus keeping to the principle of natural positioning to avoid stress. Either style is incorrect if the horse is forced to work unnaturally.

Beauty is in the eyes of the beholder. Who is to say which style looks better?

So while many styles of riding are seen in the western show ring, the horse is always asked to perform exercises exactly as prescribed by the show rules.

One of the most popular classes is the western pleasure class, in which the horse must work at the walk, jog, and lope. The natural western rider encourages his horse to walk freely, covering lots of ground. Originally, the western horse was a working animal and would have been virtually useless to the cowboy if he had walked slowly, with short strides.

The jog is a learned gait. It should move the rider along faster than the walk, yet it should be just as comfortable for today's riders as it was when it was the principal working gait of the cowboy.

The lope should be a definite three-beat gait which moves the horse at an even faster pace than the jog. However, the lope must be slow enough to be comfortable for the rider and not too tiring for the horse.

Since every horse is built differently and has a different way of moving, every horse will cover ground according to his own style. It would be unnatural for a large horse and a smaller horse to cover the same amount of ground in a single stride, even though both are moving at a relaxed pace. With this in mind, the rider should not attempt to force his horse to stay behind or to keep up with another horse as they circle the show ring.

The western pleasure horse will be asked to reverse directions and work again at all three gaits. The reverse can be a simple, slow pivot on the hindquarters, or the rider may choose to make a nice half-circle, with a diameter of at least one and one-half times the length of the horse's body.

The western pleasure horse may also be asked to change gaits frequently. It is the transition from one gait to another which is watched closely by the judge. The horse should change his movement smoothly without showing any stress or unwillingness to comply with the requested gait. The rider should avoid obvious or too-forceful cues in making transitions and should gently ease the horse into the new gait.

When all horses are standing in the lineup, the rider should not hold the horse on a tight rein, but should let the horse rest, while still standing squarely and alertly.

When asked by the judge to back the horse, the rider should lift the reins to inform the horse that work is about to begin, then cue the horse to back.

A second very popular class at western shows is the trail horse class. While trail classes generally are not timed events, it is the rider's responsibility to move the western horse through the class obstacles without undue delay. The rider should not rush the horse, but neither should he let the horse assume a lazy, inattentive attitude.

In the western riding class, the horse should demonstrate the calmness, willingness, and smoothness of the western horse at serious work. The rules require the horse to pass through a gate, weave in and out of markers, make eight flying lead changes, and go over an obstacle on the ground without disruption of stride. The rider who enters this class must be gentle yet authoritative, taking and relinquishing control frequently. The difficulty in this class is that the rider is tempted to exert too much control or not enough, and if he does one or another, the horse either resists the rider's control or becomes confused and sloppy from lack of direction.

Reining classes or classes which involve working with cattle require the utmost teamwork and sharing of responsibilities. As has been stressed throughout this book, the rider must communicate clearly to the horse what is desired and then, upon recognizing that the horse understands, immediately relinquish control to the horse, which can then complete the work with speed and form.

Fortunately, in most western shows approved by breed associations, there is no such thing as the "equitation" class. Such classes are most frequently seen at open shows.

Equitation is most commonly defined as horsemanship, and horsemanship should be defined as a rider's ability to correctly request and get a horse to perform. On the open show circuit this is not the case. Equitation horses simply walk, jog, and lope around the rail. The rider is judged, mistakenly, on his or her erect, stiff, unyielding position, attire, and the amount of silver the horse carries. It is a fact that when open-circuit competitors talk of "equitation" horses, they mean a horse which will perform as a machine, without brilliance or mistakes, so that the rider can finish the class without moving. The riders don't ride, they sit like steel rods. It is not uncommon for competitors to have a "pleasure" horse, an "equitation" horse, and a "working" horse.

In all western classes at breed-approved shows, the horse rather than the rider is judged. There is often a "horseman-

Natural western riding has its rewards.

ship" class for youth in which both horse and rider are judged. In the horsemanship class, unlike the equitation class, the horse is expected to work a pattern, demonstrating a flying change of leads, a rollback, a spin, a pivot, or some combination of such exercises. The horsemanship class is a much better test of a youth's ability to ride, and the rider who uses the natural western riding method will get the best performance.

The natural western rider will seldom succeed in today's misdefined "equitation" class; for the natural western rider is alive, working, and a part of the action.

In any competition where a judge determines the placings, there are differences of opinion. What one judge thinks is superior about the way a horse and rider work together, another judge may not find impressive. What one judge prefers in riding style, another will dislike.

Fads, styles, and fashions will come and go. What wins today may lose tomorrow.

The correct way of doing something and winning are not synonymous, and certainly the adoption of the principles of natural western riding will not guarantee blue ribbons in the show ring. But the western rider who uses the natural seat has the best chance of guaranteeing his horse the freedom and opportunity to perform brilliantly — if the horse has such ability.

The natural western rider recognizes the physical and psychological limitations of the horse and chooses not to employ force or create unnecessary stress to achieve results.

Instead, the natural western rider chooses to be no more than an equal partner to the exciting talents of the western horse at work.